Alternative Medicine

Is It for You?

Issues in Focus

Alternative Medicine
Is It for You?

Kathiann M. Kowalski

Enslow Publishers, Inc.

44 Fadem Road	PO Box 38
Box 699	Aldershot
Springfield, NJ 07081	Hants GU12 6BP
USA	UK

This book is dedicated to my daughter,
Laura Kathryn Meissner.

Library of Congress Cataloging-in-Publication Data

Kowalski, Kathiann M.
    Alternative medicine : is it for you? / Kathiann M. Kowalski.
        p. cm. — (Issues in focus)
    Includes bibliographical references and index.
    Summary: Analyzes different types of alternative medicine
practiced today, such as homeopathy, chiropractic, herbal, and
nutritional therapies, and discusses how to make an informed
decision about medical care.
    ISBN 0-89490-955-X
    1. Alternative medicine—Juvenile literature. [1. Alternative
medicine.] I. Title. II. Series: Issues in focus (Springfield, N.J.)
R733.K65   1998
615.5—dc21   98-12676
                                       CIP
                                       AC

Printed in the United States of America

10 9 8 7 6 5 4 3 2

Illustration Credits: Boiron, p. 32; Kathiann M. Kowalski,
pp. 10, 19, 22, 25, 29, 45, 47, 57, 58, 60, 64, 66, 69, 80,
85; James Morse, Bastyr University, Seattle, Washington, p. 50;
Courtesy, Archives, Palmer College of Chiropractic, p. 36;
Courtesy, Carole Rogers, University of Technology, Sydney,
Australia, p. 54; Printed with permission from the Rolf Institute
of Structural Integration, p. 77.

Cover Illustration: Kathiann M. Kowalski.

Contents

Note

Nothing in this book is intended or should be construed as medical advice. Although stories in this book reflect actual patients' experiences with alternative medicine, names have been changed to protect the privacy of patients and their families.

Acknowledgments

The author gratefully acknowledges the assistance and insights she received from the following people: Katherine Bersheim, Boiron Inc., Newtown Square, Pennsylvania; Paula Brinkman; Dean Campbell, Ayurvedic Foundations, Sandy, Utah; Robert Carroll, Sacramento City College; Karna K. Handy, The Rolf Institute, Boulder, Colorado; David and Marge Lanzola; Jenna Nash and Glenda Wiese, Palmer College of Chiropractic, Davenport, Iowa; Carole Rogers, University of Technology, Sydney; Terri Silver, Bastyr University, Seattle, Washington; my husband, Mike Meissner; and my teenage children, Chris, Laura and Bethany Meissner.

1

In Search of a Better Way

A Hopeless Case?

As an anesthesiologist and administrator at a Philadelphia hospital, Toby knew modern medicine can cure many illnesses that were once thought to be hopeless. But he knew even the most successful medical treatments don't come with guarantees.[1]

Then X rays showed tumors in Toby's body. The forty-six-year-old doctor had prostate cancer, and it had spread to his bones. Doctors gave Toby at most three years to live.[2]

Extensive surgery removed many of the tumors. Hormone therapy aimed to slow further spreading of the cancer.

7

Despite regular doses of medicine, Toby was in constant pain.

On the way home from his father's funeral in New Jersey, Toby met Sean, who had recently graduated from a natural foods cooking school in Boston. As they talked, Toby confided about his illness. "You know," said Sean, "you don't have to die, Doc."[3]

Sean told Toby about macrobiotics—a health program that holds that diet is both the cause and cure of many diseases. Toby initially dismissed the idea as being nonsense. But he was desperate.

Soon, he found himself at the Philadelphia East West Foundation, a macrobiotics educational center. The staff advised Toby to follow a strict macrobiotic diet. Instead of meat, dairy products, and processed foods, he ate brown rice, other whole grains, vegetables, soybeans, seaweed, and soup. Toby still questioned whether the foundation's directors were oversimplifying the cause of his disease. Yet he followed the diet religiously.

Then, one morning, Toby's back pain was gone. Intestinal problems gradually subsided, and Toby felt stronger each day. Where his body had been riddled with tumors one year before, computerized scans now detected no cancer. Toby was overjoyed.[4]

Several years after Toby's doctors declared that the cancer was in permanent remission, it reappeared. Toby lived longer than doctors had predicted. Nonetheless, cancer finally killed him.[5]

Spontaneous remission is the term doctors use

when a disease, such as cancer, seems to disappear on its own. Was the initial disappearance of Toby's cancer spontaneous? Was the recovery caused by his unusual diet? Or did the surgeries and hormone therapy somehow stimulate his immune system to outperform his doctors' expectations? Why did the cancer finally come back?

A Miracle Medicine?

Julie had had joint pains and vision problems ever since she was fourteen years old. As she grew older, Julie felt tingling, weakness, and occasional numbness in her legs. When she was twenty-nine, doctors finally gave Julie's condition a name: MS.

MS is multiple sclerosis, a disease of the nervous system. The majority of people afflicted are women, and most experience their first symptoms in their twenties and thirties. From time to time symptoms subside, but eventually MS comes back. Each bout is usually worse than the one before. Finally, formerly vital adults become wheelchair-bound and disabled.

Knowing this, Julie was ready to turn anywhere for help. Finally, she met a California medical doctor who also practiced homeopathy. Homeopathic physicians believe that disease can be cured by tiny amounts of natural substances that, in larger doses, would produce symptoms like those of the patient's illness. Julie's doctor prescribed an extremely dilute mixture of hemlock canian, a chemical that is usually

Fresh vegetables are part of a healthful diet, but can they cure cancer and other diseases?

toxic. Hemlock canian is not approved by the U.S. Food and Drug Administration (FDA) for treating MS.

About a month later, Julie felt better. Her vision cleared. Her energy increased. Her joints didn't ache anymore.

When this case was reported, Julie had been symptom-free for six months.[6] Was her case a remarkable cure? Or would the disease return to haunt her? Either way, how much of Julie's recovery was due to the homeopathic remedy?

Take Eighteen Pills and Call Me in the Morning

Jason was skeptical about cures from healers who aren't certified medical doctors. He went to an

Oriental medicine clinic in Woodside, New York, and told the staff about minor health conditions, such as thinning hair, a gum condition, and cold hands and feet during the winter. The clinic operator said Jason suffered from a "severe deficiency of *chi*," or universal life energy, in the spleen. Then he emptied 128 herbal tablets from a container labeled "Ginseng and Astragalus Combination" into a plastic bag and urged Jason to take six pills three times a day. Jason paid $45 for the tablets and followed the directions, but he noticed no change in his condition, no burst of energy, and no miracle cure.[7]

What, if anything, did the clinic operator diagnose? What were the pills supposed to have done? Why didn't they "work"?

What Is Alternative Medicine?

The names in these and other stories in this book have been changed to protect the privacy of patients and their families, but each case tells about a real person's experience with alternative medicine. When established medicine offers little hope, millions of people turn to unproven, yet enticing, treatments.

In this book, "alternative medicine" means a practice or treatment that is

- intended to address and improve a health condition;

- is not generally taught in U.S. medical schools; and

- is not generally accepted by most medical

doctors as supported by sufficient scientific documentation of safety and effectiveness against specific diseases or health conditions.

Although alternative medicine is not accepted by most medical doctors, millions use it to seek relief for everything from minor discomforts to major illnesses. *The New England Journal of Medicine* reported that one in three patients used some form of alternative therapy in 1990. Yet while four-fifths of those patients used conventional medicine at the same time, they did not tell their doctors about the alternative treatments.[8]

Does alternative medicine work? Many practitioners and their patients maintain that treatments can improve health less expensively and sometimes more effectively than conventional medical treatments. The National Institutes of Health (NIH) has funded limited studies examining acupuncture, hypnosis, imagery, and other therapies.

Meanwhile, the FDA warns that some treatments sold as "alternative medicine" are deliberately deceptive. Teenagers and the elderly are two groups who are especially targeted by health fraud.[9]

Questions to Ask Yourself

How are alternative therapies supposed to work? Can you tell which treatments offer a real possibility for healing and which are just hype? This book brings these issues into focus by examining some of the dozens of alternative therapies available today.

This is by no means a how-to book. It does not

offer medical advice. It is not a recommendation or endorsement of any treatment. Instead, this book helps you understand claims advanced by proponents of several therapies along with concerns expressed by critics. And you will move farther along the path to becoming an informed health care consumer.

2

Conventional versus Alternative Medicine

Biomedicine is what we know as "conventional" medicine. Biomedicine sees bacteria, viruses, fungi, and other organic agents as the cause of many—but not all—diseases. It uses vaccines, drugs, and other medications to ward off the effects of those biological invaders.

Although biomedicine is termed *conventional* today, it became dominant in Western health care only within the past two hundred years. On a global view, different medical systems dominate in other cultures.[1]

Ancient Origins

Hailed as the father of Western medicine, the ancient Greek physician Hippocrates (460–377 B.C.) systematically studied the human body and healing arts. Yet when it came to explaining how people get sick, Hippocrates and the ancient Greeks saw the body as being at the mercy of four forces, or "humors": air, water, fire, and earth. When the humors were out of balance, these ancient doctors reasoned, sickness followed.

Passing centuries brought improvements, such as quarantine procedures to contain infectious diseases after the bubonic plague swept Europe in the thirteenth century. When the French philosopher René Descartes (1596–1650) introduced the idea of thinking about the mind and body as separate, scientists began asking more questions about individual body functions and diseases. Still, the humor theory prevailed.[2]

In colonial America, doctors' supposed cures for disease included treatments that seem barbaric today. Patients were routinely bled or made to suffer bites from blood-sucking leeches. Ground beetles were used to cause blisters and draw out "bad vapors." Strong laxatives were given to purge, or cleanse, the system by diarrhea. Emetics caused vomiting. If the disease didn't kill the patient, the doctor's healing efforts often would![3]

Practically anyone could charge patients for "treatments" without having to prove their safety or effectiveness. Throughout the nineteenth century, people with little, if any, science training called themselves "doctor." Even the relatively few physicians with a university education lacked basic knowledge about microorganisms and infections.

Not knowing that germs cause infections, early medical doctors had little or no regard for sanitary procedure. In contrast to the latex gloves, masks, and scrub suits of today's sterile operating room, doctors took few measures to ensure cleanliness. Outbreaks of typhoid, smallpox, cholera, and other diseases were frequent.

Germs of Modern Biomedicine

By the mid-nineteenth century, things started changing. The French scientist Louis Pasteur discovered that microorganisms can cause disease. His medicine to prevent rabies, a fatal disease of the central nervous system that is caught from infected mammals, was one of the first vaccines. Pasteur also urged people to boil milk to kill harmful bacteria, a process today known as pasteurization.

Western doctors gradually accepted the "germ theory" of disease. This theory holds that microorganisms, such as bacteria, fungi, and viruses, cause many diseases.

Other scientists focused on the ways patients became infected by microorganisms. The Scottish doctor Joseph Lister used carbolic acid spray to kill bacteria and combat high rates of surgical infection. Over time, antiseptic procedures, such as surgical gowns, masks, gloves, and sterilized instruments, became standard medical practice.

During the twentieth century, scientists learned more about microorganisms. Gradually, they developed vaccines to prevent many diseases and antibiotics to combat bacterial infections.

Other changes occurred too. By advocating strict standards for medical education and practice, the American Medical Association (organized in 1846) sought to stamp out bad practices that not only failed to heal but also gave the medical profession a bad name. About the same time, Harvard University and other universities upgraded their curricula to emphasize new discoveries in biomedicine.

By the 1870s, many states had set up boards of health. In 1888 the U.S. Supreme Court upheld an 1882 West Virginia law requiring doctors to have a degree from a reputable medical school in order to practice medicine.[4]

What was "reputable" remained a subject of debate. In 1910, educator Abraham Flexner authored a report, commonly called the Flexner Report, that set strict, biomedicine-oriented standards for United States medical schools. Schools meeting the standards prospered. Those that did not—including some that taught theories similar to some of today's alternative health practices—closed.[5]

On the one hand, the Flexner Report provided some quality control for medical schools, so patients could trust that medical school graduates met basic requirements. However, long after its publication, the report helped keep many women and people of color from being admitted to medical schools. And practitioners of some types of alternative medicine say the report unfairly limited consumers' access to different types of treatment.

Thus, conventional medicine became biomedicine—the style practiced by doctors with either an M.D. (medical doctor) or a D.O. (doctor of osteopathy) degree. Osteopathic doctors' education is similar to that of the medical doctors in many respects, but training places more stress on musculoskeletal functions and certain treatments involving physical manipulation of the body.[6] M.D.'s and D.O.'s are still the only types of practitioners licensed in all fifty states to practice medicine. "Practicing medicine" means performing general surgery and prescribing medications for all sorts of illnesses.

Achievements of Modern Medicine

Biomedicine is perhaps proudest of its success in combating infectious, or contagious, diseases. Thanks to vaccinations, smallpox has been wiped out—literally, it is a thing of the past. World Health Organization officials expect polio to be wiped out by the year 2000.[7]

As of 1996, 80 percent of children worldwide were receiving immunization against childhood diseases such as measles, tuberculosis, diphtheria, tetanus, whooping cough, and polio. The World

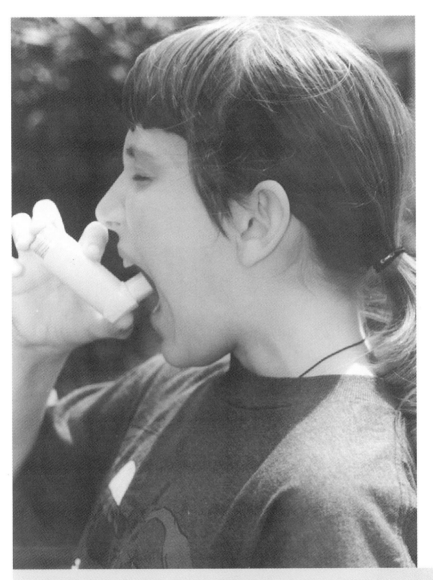

This girl relies on the drugs in prescription inhalers to suppress her asthma symptoms. Such medications enable millions of people with potentially life-threatening conditions to lead normal, active lives.

Health Organization reports that each year, immunization prevents the deaths of 3 million children and saves an additional 750,000 from crippling disabilities.[8]

High-tech imaging and new surgery techniques help doctors save more lives than ever before. Other medical milestones focus on the fight against cancer, an illness that strikes about one-third of all Americans at some time in their lives. Early detection, surgery, chemotherapy, and radiation therapy have boosted survival rates higher than ever. Biomedicine is also searching for cures for AIDS and other diseases.

Doctors practicing conventional medicine vigorously urge patients to follow a healthy lifestyle. Eating a balanced diet, exercising regularly, and avoiding unhealthy behaviors like smoking and using drugs reduces the risk of heart attacks, cancer, and other serious diseases.

Disenchantment

With all these wonderful accomplishments, why are some people turning to alternative medicine? As biomedicine has become more high-tech, it has also become more impersonal. The general practitioner who made house calls is a thing of the past. Today's medical profession is divided into specialties and subspecialties: cardiologists, oncologists, surgeons, gynecologists, and so forth. Even "family medicine" has become a board-certified specialty.

At the same time, medical costs have soared. Some people cannot afford conventional medical care. Other people may have health plans but get wrapped up in "red tape" while awaiting authorizations for specialist referrals or non-emergency surgery.

Meanwhile, consumer activism and an increasing trend toward litigation highlight inadequacies. Some patients seem to be helpless victims of incompetence, like the Florida man who woke up to find that doctors had amputated the wrong foot.

Even when care is competent, biomedicine has less than spectacular results with certain health problems. While millions of people suffer from short-term low back pain, for example, studies suggest that neither surgery nor long-term medication is more effective than certain alternative therapies or over-the-counter pain relievers coupled with mild exercise.[9]

Ask alternative practitioners about conventional medicine, and you will hear more criticism. Some alternative practitioners and conventional doctors cooperate and refer patients to each other. But many alternative practitioners feel medical doctors jealously guard their health care territory. They believe physicians have a vested interest in rejecting new ideas that clash with medical school teaching. They claim most doctors are set in their ways and unwilling to undergo training in different treatments that would be less costly to the patient (and likely also less profitable for the practitioner).[10]

Behind the turf wars are philosophical differences. Alternative practitioners often refer to biomedicine as "allopathic," meaning it focuses primarily on diseases and symptoms. Many drugs prescribed by conventional doctors suppress symptoms, making the patient feel better. A decongestant, for example, makes your nose stop running when you have a cold.

But alternative therapies like homeopathy say symptoms are signs that the body is trying to heal itself. Other therapies, like Ayurveda and acupuncture, are based on the theory that symptoms signal that the body's vital energy is out of balance. Instead of suppressing symptoms, these therapies claim to

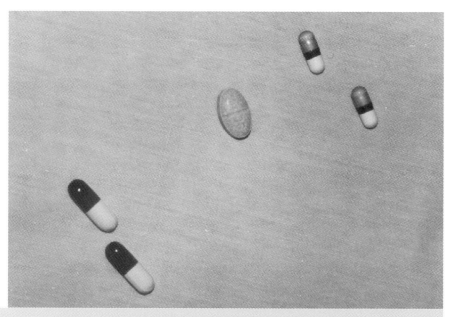

These conventional medicines are typically used to suppress flu symptoms. Shown are single adult doses of a fever reducer, a decongestant, and an antihistamine.

address the underlying cause of illness and to treat the whole person—an approach commonly called "holism."

Alternative practitioners also dislike the harsh side effects that sometimes accompany treatment with conventional drugs. They claim that their treatments address health problems "gently" and "naturally."

Prove It!

Conventional medicine's primary response to alternative medicine's claims can be summed up in two words: Prove it![11]

Advocates of conventional medicine want more than testimonials from one, twelve, or even one thousand people that "it works for me." They demand hard scientific proof—proof developed through rigidly designed studies with significant numbers of patients and controls to protect against bias and chance results.

Moreover, critics of alternative medicine want the studies to be published in peer-reviewed journals with strict editorial standards. Peer review means that experts critique studies in search of errors and inconsistencies. The paper is published only after it has addressed the experts' criticisms.

Why insist on scientific proof? Suppose Laura has a twenty-four-hour virus. Moaning in pain, she drags herself to an experimental clinic and receives a "mystery treatment." The next day, Laura feels better, but the virus would have been over by then anyway. Because she felt better after seeing the practitioner, Laura may think alternative medicine cured her. This is called post hoc rationalization.

Other "cures" occur for unknown reasons—a condition called spontaneous remission. Some—but not all—of these happy patients may use an alternative therapy, but there is no proof that the alternative therapy caused the remission.

Then there is the power of suggestion. If you expect that medicine from a doctor will make you better, you may perceive that the medicine is working—even if it is only a "placebo," such as a colored sugar pill. Studies have shown this placebo effect generally produces improvement in one-third, and sometimes up to nearly two-thirds, of all patients.[12]

So, how do scientists know whether a cure works? One way is to use double-blind tests. One large group of patients gets the medicine being tested while another large group gets a sham medicine, such as a sugar pill. Neither the patients nor the people handing out the pills know who gets the real medicine. Afterward, results are compared.

If the group that took real medicine improves more than the control group, more analysis follows. Statistical calculations test whether results would have occurred by chance.

Studies are then reported in professional, peer-reviewed journals. Publication lets other professionals know what is going on. It also provides an opportunity to repeat tests to see whether other researchers obtain the same results.

Publication of research in peer-reviewed journals gives experts in the field an opportunity to scrutinize studies to protect against bias or methodology flaws.

Federal law requires manufacturers of new drugs for conventional medicine to prove that they are safe and effective. Biomedicine's advocates say alternative medicine should have to meet the same standards. Even when "natural" therapies do not affirmatively harm the patient, skeptics claim alternative practitioners should not be allowed to profit from peddling ineffective cures—a practice called quackery.

Beyond this, conventional medicine criticizes different alternatives as relying on mysticism and superstition rather than on hard scientific proof.

After finally smashing the ancient humor theory, modern biomedicine's advocates worry about any approach that harkens back to those origins.

Here to Stay?

Despite criticisms, alternative practitioners say they offer patients a viable choice in health care. And many patients swear that alternative medicine helps them feel better!

The next chapters look at a few of the many therapies available under the heading of alternative medicine. With health care being a multibillion-dollar industry, there is a lot of money at stake. Beyond this, the debate directly affects the lives of millions of people who choose either conventional or alternative medicine.

Homeopathy and Chiropractic

Can crushed bees cure what ails you? How about onions? Or tarantulas? Maybe squid ink or dissolved poison ivy can help. These odd ingredients are among the hundreds of substances used in homeopathy.

Homeopathy: Like Cures Like

Appalled by bloodletting and other treatments used by conventional medicine in the 1700s, German physician Samuel Hahnemann (1755–1843) turned to natural substances to explore their healing qualities. Hahnemann's early experiments focused on Peruvian bark. It contains

27

quinine, a drug used to treat malaria. Malaria is a feverish illness common in damp areas where insects breed.

Hahnemann administered Peruvian bark to himself, even though he didn't have malaria. Soon he had a fever, rapid pulse, thirst, and other malaria symptoms. From this, Hahnemann developed his "law of similars": *Similia similibus curantur,* or "Like cures like."

While conventional medicine aimed to suppress symptoms, Hahnemann saw them as the body's natural efforts to restore order. By administering a small amount of a substance that can produce symptoms like those of an illness, homeopathic doctors believe that they stimulate the body's ability to cure itself.

Hahnemann then studied other substances, such as mercury, arsenic, and belladonna. These studies, or provings, gave test subjects (often Hahnemann's family and friends) repeated doses until they showed symptoms similar to different diseases.

Since strong concentrations had toxic, or poisonous, effects, Hahnemann reasoned that dilute amounts would produce healing effects. The more dilute a solution was, he believed, the greater its curing powers would be.[1]

While the process has changed somewhat over the years, the manufacture of homeopathic medicines still follows basic steps taught by Hahnemann. For plants or soluble materials, the manufacturer begins with a concentrated extract. Insoluble

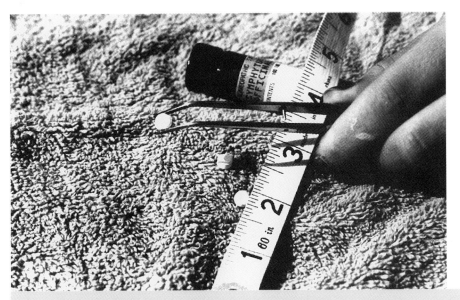

Derived from the comfrey plant, the homeopathic remedy Symphytum officinalis *is often used to treat joint pains and to promote healing after broken bones have been set. While many remedies come in liquid form, tablets like this also can be bought without prescription at health food stores and drugstore chains.*

materials like copper or other metals are ground with milk sugar for three hours to produce a fine powder.

The extract or powder is diluted to 1x—a concentration of one part extract to 10 parts of water or alcohol. A 1x solution is diluted again to 2x, or a ratio of one part extract to 100 parts liquid. The process is repeated over and over to reach dilutions of 6x (1:1 million), 9x (1:1 billion), 30x, or even 60x. At each step, the liquid solution is shaken forcefully.[2]

Homeopathic medicines are sold as both liquids

and as tablets. For tablets, the diluted liquid medicine has been added to sugar. A dose of homeopathic medicine can be as small as a single drop or one tiny tablet.

The specific remedy for any ailment depends on the individual's complete symptom picture, including tastes, cravings, and moods. A conventional doctor typically takes your pulse and blood pressure and asks what's bothering you. A homeopath probes further. What foods do you like? Are you easily angered? Do you crave fresh air? Depending on the answers, an allergy sufferer might get a very dilute preparation of *Apis* (crushed bee) or a medicine derived from plants, such as *Euphrasia* (eyebright), *Urtica urens* (stinging nettle), or *Allium cepa* (red onion).[3] A child with an earache might get *Pulsatilla* (a homeopathic medicine prepared from spoiled meat), an herb-based medicine like *Chamomila* (the flowering plant chamomile), or extremely dilute medicines derived from poisonous plants, such as *Belladonna* (deadly nightshade) or *Aconite* (monkshood).[4]

An Impossible Cure?

Part of homeopathy's appeal is that its medicines come from natural substances—plants, animals, and minerals. Many "conventional" medicines are also prepared from natural substances, such as penicillin (derived from bread mold). Yet Hahnemann's theory that "less is more" is the exact opposite of what conventional medicine teaches.

Conventional medicine relies on the dose-response relationship. The dose-response relationship presumes that the more there is of a chemical to which an organism is exposed, the more intense will be the chemical's effects. For practically all chemicals, pharmacologists (scientists who make conventional medicines) believe that an organism must be exposed to a minimum, or threshold, concentration for there to be any effect at all.

For example, if you take the recommended dose of an over-the-counter medicine like aspirin, your headache will probably feel better soon. If you smash a tablet and take only one grain, however, you will not do your headache any good. Too many tablets will make you ill.

Homeopathy not only disregards this notion of threshold concentrations and dose-response relationship but also assumes a medicine can cure even after it is no longer "there." By the time a homeopathic remedy is diluted to 24x, there is only a one in ten chance that a single molecule of the original extract remains in the mixture. For greater dilutions like 30x and 60x, the chances are next to nothing.

A 1994 report by *Consumer Reports* criticized homeopathy's theoretical underpinnings as "highly implausible."[5] William Jarvis, a medical school professor who has served as president of the National Council Against Health Fraud, has said, "Homeopathy represents a totally ridiculous approach to pharmacology."[6]

But advocates like Sarah Richardson, who has

served as director of the Society of Homeopaths in Great Britain, maintain that homeopathic solutions can aid in restoring health. She suggests that mixing and shaking solutions during manufacturing imparts qualities of the curing substance's molecular structure to the medium in which it is diluted.[7]

"We don't know the mechanism by which these drugs act," admits Edward Chapman of the American Institute of Homeopathy, "but we don't know how lots of drugs work."[8] Meanwhile, studies are under way. Questions Chapman has been investigating include whether homeopathic remedies can help treat cases of mild traumatic brain injury.[9]

Most homeopathic medicines are manufactured according to precise methods. Shown here is the Lyon, France, headquarters of Boiron, one of the world's largest manufacturers of homeopathic medicines.

In 1994, Jennifer Jacobs, a medical doctor and homeopath, studied children with diarrhea. Those who got both conventional treatment (fluids with water, sugar, and salt) plus tiny doses of homeopathic medicine recovered faster than children in a control group who had only conventional treatment.[10] Another study in Glasgow, Scotland, concluded that homeopathic medicines effectively relieve hay fever.[11]

Even when a trial suggests support for homeopathy's effectiveness, however, different results may occur when other researchers repeat the study. This raises questions about what, if anything, either study proves.

Other studies conduct a "metanalysis," reviewing results of dozens of studies. However, scientists disagree about whether such analyses improperly compare "apples and oranges" and about whether they show that homeopathy is effective or ineffective overall.[12]

Medical school professor and internist Thomas Delbanco has questioned whether homeopathy may rely largely on the placebo effect.[13] In other words, do people feel better after homeopathic medicines because they expect to be cured?

While the debate continues, Americans spend more than $200 million annually for homeopathic remedies.[14] "What I have seen in my homeopathic work is that it really does seem to help people get better," says Jacobs. "I'm not saying I can cure everyone but I do see where people's overall health is improved over the course of treatment."[15]

Chiropractic's Controversial History

Pop! Crack! To some people, these are the sounds of a champagne bottle opening or a twig snapping. For many patients, these words describe the noise they hear when a chiropractor adjusts their back.

When David Eisenberg of the Harvard Medical School and his colleagues surveyed people about alternative medicine, 10 percent said they had used chiropractic within the past year.[16] In the United States, approximately fifty thousand chiropractors treat patients by manually repositioning the vertebrae—the twenty-four bones that surround the spinal cord—and by using other techniques.[17]

Modern chiropractic dates back just over one hundred years to 1895. Daniel David (D.D.) Palmer (1845–1913) practiced as a "magnetic healer" (one who offered to cure by the laying on of hands) in Davenport, Iowa. Palmer had previously been a beekeeper, fish peddler, and grocer. He never attended medical school, but he had read widely about anatomy and illness.

On September 18, 1895, Palmer examined Harvey Lillard, a janitor who "had been so deaf for 17 years that he could not hear the racket of a wagon on the street or the ticking of a watch."[18] In examining the man's spine he found "a vertebra racked from its normal position." According to Palmer, a "half-hour's talk persuaded Mr. Lillard to allow me to replace it. I racked it into position by using the spinous process as a lever and soon the man could hear as before."[19]

Critics question whether the account was exaggerated, since the nerves that control hearing are in the brain, not in the back.[20] Regardless of how and to what extent Lillard was cured, Palmer was encouraged. One early patient, Samuel Weed, helped Palmer coin the term *chiropractic* from Greek words meaning "done by hand." In 1897, Palmer established the Palmer Infirmary and Chiropractic Institute in Davenport, Iowa.[21]

In 1902, Palmer's son, Bartlett Joshua (B.J.) Palmer (1882–1961), graduated from his father's school. For a short period, B.J. helped his father run the school. Then in 1906, the elder Palmer was jailed for twenty-three days and fined $500 for practicing medicine without a license. Soon after, he left to establish chiropractic schools in Oklahoma and Oregon.

B.J. Palmer retained control of the Davenport school and promoted chiropractic vigorously. He developed various innovations, including a machine to pinpoint "subluxations."

In chiropractic, a "subluxation" is a misalignment of the spine. B.J. and various other chiropractors believed that such misalignments could impair transmission of "nerve energy." This, in turn, would inhibit the body's "innate intelligence," meaning its ability to maintain good health.[22]

Chiropractors who adopted B.J.'s philosophy and

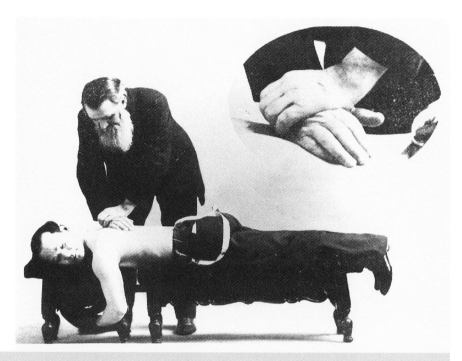

D.D. Palmer, the founder of chiropractic, adjusts a patient's spine, circa 1906.

practiced only his recommended therapies were called "straights." Other practitioners, called "mixers," used other treatments as well.

Effective lobbying by chiropractic groups led all fifty states to establish chiropractic licensing boards. Strong lobbying also persuaded Congress to allow coverage of chiropractic care under the Medicare program.[23] Nonetheless, from the 1930s to the 1970s, the American Medical Association (AMA) either discouraged or outright forbade physicians from referring patients to chiropractors.

In 1976, Chester Wilk and other chiropractors filed an antitrust lawsuit, *Wilk* v. *American Medical Association*, in the United States District Court for the Northern District of Illinois. Eleven years later, in 1987, Judge Susan Getzendanner held that the AMA and two other groups acted illegally by encouraging boycotts of chiropractors.[24] She never decided whether chiropractic "works," but chiropractors applauded her ruling.[25]

Oh, My Aching Back

The majority of complaints handled by chiropractors involve back pain, which is a problem for up to 75 percent of Americans at one time or another. Nutritionist Kurt Butler, who founded a consumer-advocacy group called Quackery Action Council, has argued that treating subluxations, or misalignments of the spine, is too subjective because diagnosis can vary from one chiropractor to another.[26] But in 1992, the Rand Corporation reported that spinal manipulation therapies, including chiropractic, were more effective than surgery for relieving certain kinds of back pain.[27]

Then, in December 1994, the Agency for Health Care Policy and Research (AHCPR), which is part of the U.S. Public Health Service, issued guidelines for treating acute (short-term) low back pain. Recommended treatments included over-the-counter pain relievers, moderate exercise (walking, swimming, or biking), exercises for trunk muscles, and "spinal manipulation."[28]

The American Chiropractic Association praised these and similar studies. Indeed, even if a person is not in pain, many chiropractors recommend regular adjustments to minimize health problems and correct subluxations before they become serious.[29]

Meanwhile, critics like George Magner, founder of Victims of Chiropractic, claim that chiropractors exaggerated the AHCPR findings.[30] They also argue there is no evidence that regular "maintenance" adjustments to the spine improve health.[31] Nonetheless, many people, including chiropractors themselves, say they feel better by having their backs adjusted regularly.

Chiropractors must take at least six years of college and graduate courses before becoming licensed. Required courses include anatomy and other medical subjects. Should chiropractors be relied on as "family doctors" to treat various medical conditions beyond backaches and muscle pains?

Some chiropractors, such as members of the National Association for Chiropractic Medicine, treat only musculoskeletal problems. Yet brochures and charts in some other chiropractors' offices suggest that the therapy's ability to restore order in the body can help with conditions that appear unrelated to the spine, such as epilepsy, impotency, and allergies. After collecting and reviewing such brochures, the writers of *Consumer Reports* said they lack a proven scientific basis.[32]

Yet many patients believe chiropractic can help with a host of problems. One Vermont woman, who used to have irregular menstrual cycles, praised chiropractic, saying, "Aside from achieving a much-wanted pregnancy, I have fewer headaches than I had prior to being under chiropractic care."[33] Whether she would have become pregnant anyway is unknown. Rigorous, double-blind studies cannot be done on a single patient in either conventional or alternative medicine.

Is It Safe?

Critic George Magner, founder of Victims of Chiropractic, claims chiropractors perform dangerous maneuvers without warning patients about inherent risks until it is too late. For example, Magner says that sudden rotation of the neck can injure arteries and interrupt the flow of blood to the brain.[34] He cites the case of a forty-four-year-old mother who suffered a stroke after a chiropractor manipulated her neck.[35] Other risks that Magner feels should be disclosed to patients in advance include bone fractures, injured nerves, ruptured disks, soft-tissue injuries, overuse of X rays, and potential failure to diagnose a more serious problem.[36]

In his book *Everybody's Guide to Chiropractic Health Care*, however, chiropractor Nathaniel Altman claims the profession has an outstanding safety record. In contrast with malpractice cases in conventional medicine, he argues, chiropractic has few cases of poor judgment and serious injury.[37]

To counter criticisms about overexposure to X rays, chiropractors say they are necessary to rule out serious medical problems. Many practitioners use screens, shields, high-speed film, and other measures, which are similar to precautions used by conventional medical doctors and dentists.[38]

Other issues fuel the debate, such as whether chiropractic is appropriate for very young children.[39] Meanwhile, more than ten years after the *Wilk* decision, some physicians and chiropractors are showing greater cooperation toward each other. In chiropractor Steve Campbell's view, "Physicians and chiropractors have to work together to help the patient."[40]

4

Alternative Medicine from India and China

Ayurveda (ah-yer-VAY-da) means "science of life" in ancient Sanskrit. Drawing on Hindu traditions, texts, and practices that date as far back as five thousand years, Ayurveda strives to achieve wellness through how a person lives: diet, exercise, outlook, cleansing, and meditation.

Ayurveda—India's "Science of Life"

The vital energy behind life and healing in Ayurveda is called prana (PRAN-ah). Ancient Hindu philosophers in India taught that energy is the source of all matter. Matter in turn is divided into five basic elements: earth, air, fire, water, and ether (or space). Combinations of the elements in the body produce three humors, or forces, called doshas (DOH-shahs). These forces—vata, pitta, and kapha—are believed to govern all physical and mental functions.[1]

Vata (VAY-ta) is supposed to control body functions associated with movement. These include blood circulation, brain functions, muscular movement, waste excretion, some nerves, breathing, anxiety, grief, and enthusiasm.

Pitta (PITT-ah) is associated with fire. It is said to control functions such as body heat, digestion, hunger, thirst, vision, cheerfulness, intellect, and luster in the body's appearance.

Kapha (KUFF-ah) is associated with the earth and water elements. Kapha is said to control the sinuses, chest and throat, secretions, and certain emotions.[2]

Ayurveda categorizes people's prakriti (PRUKK-er-tee), or mind-body type, according to which dosha or doshas dominate. There are vata, pitta, and kapha types, along with vata-pitta, pitta-kapha, vata-kapha, and vata-pitta-kapha types.

Descriptions of mind-body types get very detailed. *In Boundless Energy: The Complete Mind/Body Program for Overcoming Chronic Fatigue*, Ayurveda proponent and medical doctor Deepak Chopra observes that pitta types often have fair or ruddy skin and blond, red, or light brown hair. They hate wasting time. If dinner is slightly late, they are ravenous. They have a determined stride and often feel they should take command of situations.[3]

By studying mind-body types and examining a person's current condition, practitioners seek to identify imbalances in vata, pitta, and kapha. Ayurvedic theory claims that emotions, like repressed fear (affecting vata), anger (excessive pitta), or envy (aggravating kapha) can lead to imbalances. Or imbalances can result from actions outside the body, such as stress, inappropriate foods, weather, or environmental toxins. Ayurveda states that imbalances lead to the buildup of toxins, or ama (AH-ma), which cause symptoms and disease.[4]

Eyes, lips, nails, and the tongue are just a few of the characteristics that Ayurvedic practitioners examine to decide what kind of imbalance exists. Practitioners also take the pulse at different points to assess strengths and weaknesses of vata, pitta, and kapha.[5] Then practitioners prescribe specific diets, medicines, and behavior practices to restore balance.

Restoring Balance with Ayurveda

Practitioners of Ayurveda classify foods according to six basic tastes: sweet, sour, salty, pungent, bitter, and astringent (dry). Balancing these tastes aims to "pacify" or reduce whichever dosha is aggravated. For example, a patient diagnosed with aggravated vata and too little kapha would be told to add salty, sweet, and sour foods to the diet. At the same time, he or she would decrease the relative amounts of pungent, astringent, and bitter foods.[6]

Besides giving dietary advice, Ayurvedic practitioners prescribe medicines. Some ingredients are exotic. Others are frequently found in kitchen cupboards.

Cinnamon, for example, can be used to correct vata and kapha disorders, promote digestion, and relieve symptoms of colds, congestion, and cough. Turmeric, a spice for seafood, poultry, pasta, egg, and curry dishes, is used to promote digestion, relieve throat congestion, treat diabetes, and reduce inflammation from bruises. Other kitchen medicines in Ayurveda include ginger, honey, licorice, mustard, coriander, cloves, and cardamom.[7]

Because practitioners believe a buildup of toxins leads to disease, Ayurvedic therapy includes cleansing and purging practices that aim to force toxins out of the body. Regimens range from daily washing and massage of body points with medicinal oils to sweat treatments and cleansing nasal passages with sesame oil.[8]

More extreme practices aim to treat specific health problems. Therapeutic vomiting is used for repeated attacks of asthma, cough, and bronchitis. Vomiting is also part of Ayurvedic therapy for diabetes, epilepsy (between attacks), chronic sinus problems, and chronic indigestion.[9]

Other practices seek to eliminate toxins by stimulating bowel movements. One general method is the drinking of hot water throughout the day.[10] Other methods treat specific disorders. One laxative treatment for menstrual problems, which quickly

Ayurveda practitioners use foods from six basic taste groups to correct perceived imbalances in doshas. Examples of the taste groups are (clockwise from lower left): bitter—green leafy vegetables like spinach; pungent—cumin and other spices; astringent or dry—lentils; sour—yogurt; sweet—breads; salty—salt and salted foods.

produces several bowel movements, involves taking four teaspoons of castor oil mixed in one-fourth cup of orange juice monthly in the middle of the woman's cycle.[11] Enemas of water, sesame oil, herbs, milk, or broth are used for other ailments, such as backache, kidney stones, and arthritis.[12]

Physician-supervised bloodletting is occasionally used to treat pitta disorders. Or patients may take herbal preparations, such as burdock-root tea, to purify the blood.[13] Fasting regimens are also used periodically in Ayurveda.

Exercise and Meditation

Exercise plays an important role in Ayurvedic medicine, with the types of recommended activities varying according to the individual's mind-body type. Light exercise is deemed best for vata types, for example, while kapha types are urged to jog or do vigorous aerobic workouts.[14]

Beyond this, proponents of Ayurvedic medicine recommend yoga.[15] Besides improving muscle tone, yoga poses and breathing exercises seek to balance the doshas and strengthen internal organs. For example, the one-footed tree pose aims to tone and stretch the abdominal organs and aid digestion while improving balance and strengthening the legs. The bow pose—grasping the ankles while raising the chest and legs and balancing on the abdomen—tries to aid digestion and elimination of wastes. Other poses are used mainly for meditation, such as the cross-legged half-lotus and lotus positions.[16]

Ayurvedic practitioners strongly encourage people to meditate in order to increase self-awareness, reduce stress, and obtain inner calm. Patients may use different methods, such as sitting quietly in a yoga posture or concentrating while breathing in and out.

Transcendental Meditation, or TM, is another meditation method taught at Maharishi Ayur-Vedic

The tree pose is one of more than seven dozen yoga positions.

Health Centers in different parts of the United States. Repeating a sound, or mantra, over and over is believed to heighten awareness. Advocates say TM leads to great insights, relaxation, and significant health benefits.[17] On the other hand, TM-Ex, an organization of former meditators, claims that Transcendental Meditation doesn't deliver promised benefits and may even lead to depression, anxiety, and headaches.[18] Not surprisingly, followers of Transcendental Meditation disagree.

Criticisms of Ayurveda

Ayurveda is based on mysticism, not science, says Kurt Butler, who founded the Quackery Action Council. He thinks its mind-body types are arbitrary and simplistic. And he thinks some of Ayurveda's ideas are absurd or even potentially dangerous. For example, Butler charges that some enema solutions may introduce potentially toxic chemicals into the body.[19]

Dietitian and health writer Jack Raso complains that Ayurveda's lingo—dosha, ama, and so on—clothes traditional folk medicine with false authority. He says Ayurveda is not rooted in proven science but in mystic beliefs and in the Hindu religion.

Raso is also skeptical about products and services marketed by practitioners. Among the figures he cites are $2,500 to $4,300 per week for diagnosis and treatment at a clinic; $3,400 for meditation training; $45 for sixty herbal tablets; $95 for a month's supply of a dietary supplement;

and $2,700 to $6,600 for three weeks of annual purification treatments.[20]

Despite criticism, certain Ayurvedic practices are being scrutinized more closely. One government-funded study seeks to compare effects of an Ayurvedic health promotion program with a conventional "wellness" program. Another study looks at whether yoga can help treat heroin addiction.[21] While studies proceed, the debate between proponents and skeptics will continue.

Acupuncture: Balancing Yin and Yang

Acupuncture is a traditional Oriental medicine that focuses on the flow of vital energy, called chi (chee), throughout the body. The FDA estimates that between 9 and 12 million acupuncture treatments are performed annually in the United States.[22]

The Yellow Emperor's Classic of Internal Medicine, written twenty-five hundred years ago, sets out basic principles of acupuncture. Drawing ideas from Taoism, an Oriental philosophy, acupuncture seeks to balance yin and yang. Yin and yang represent the interplay between many types of opposites. Examples include day and night, male and female, warm and cold, and so on.

Just as opposites exist in the physical world, acupuncture theory states that yin and yang exist in the body. Generally, yin refers to concepts characterized as below/interior/contracting/resting. Examples include the front of the body, mucus, and feet.[23]

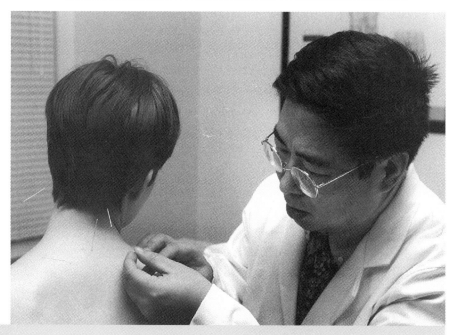

Dr. Qiang Cao gives an acupuncture treatment to a patient.

Yang concepts are considered to be above/exterior/expanding/moving. Examples are the back, arms and legs, skin, and head. Internal organs are likewise considered to be either more yin or yang, such as kidneys (yin) and bladder (yang).[24]

Besides the concepts of yin and yang, Oriental medicine teaches that the world and the body are composed of five basic elements, called wood, fire, earth, metal, and water.[25] Each element is associated with particular body organs: the liver and gallbladder with wood; the heart and small intestine with fire; the spleen and stomach with earth; the lungs and large intestine with metal; and the kidneys and bladder with water.[26]

Acupuncturists say chi flows through the body along pathways called meridians. Acupuncturists use two midline meridians and twelve primary meridians, plus collateral (supplementary) channels.[27] For example, the Spleen meridian travels along each side of the body from the toe, along the inner side of the leg, through the abdomen, and to the thorax, or chest.[28] The Triple-heater meridian starts at the ring finger and runs up the arm, over the shoulder, and around the ear to the edge of the eyebrow.[29]

Diagnosing and Treating Disruptions in Chi

Acupuncturists believe that disruptions in the flow of chi cause illness. To diagnose problems, practitioners take the patient's pulse on each wrist in three places. They believe each position reveals information about different organs: the heart and small intestine, the liver and gallbladder, the spleen and stomach, and so on.

Practitioners use their hands to probe different parts of the body. They also study the patient's tongue.[30] After forming a diagnosis, the acupuncturist seeks to redirect chi's flow by inserting thin needles at specific points throughout the body. Most acupuncturists use any of 360 main points for treating patients.[31]

In theory, gentle needle manipulation alters the flow of energy, restoring the balance between yin and yang. For example, one point on the leg, called Spleen 6, is believed to be the intersection of three yin pathways. The point is used to treat complaints such as hypertension, migraines, painful urination, and menstrual disorders.[32]

Acupuncture needles are only slightly bigger in diameter than thick hair. While some acupuncturists use sterilized reusable needles, concerns about AIDS have led many practitioners to switch to disposable needles. Patients can ask any acupuncturist to use disposable needles.[33]

Patients generally feel no pain, or at most a slight sensation of heat or tingling. While some patients report improvement after their first treatment, acupuncture often takes place over several weeks or months.[34]

As a variation of the basic method, some acupuncturists apply minor electrical impulses to needles. Others use needles only on the outer ear.[35] Still other practitioners use pea-sized wads of the herb moxa (also called mugwort) instead of needles. Burning the wad transfers heat to the acupuncture point. Other variations include acupressure and shiatsu, which stimulate points with pressure rather than needles.[36]

Many acupuncturists also direct patients to take Oriental herbs. The herbs are believed to have healing properties that help balance chi.[37]

Success—Or Suspicion?

Claims about the success of acupuncture vary widely. Carole Rogers, a professor who teaches acupuncture in Sydney, Australia, says the procedure is extremely beneficial for musculoskeletal disorders.

"By that I mean things like lower back pain, tennis elbow, knee problems, neck and shoulder tension and general muscular aches, pains and strains," she says.[38]

Other areas where Rogers feels acupuncture can help include digestive disorders, including ulcers, indigestion, and bowel problems, as well as stress-related problems like headaches, anxiety, depression, insomnia, and exhaustion. Areas where she would refer patients to conventional doctors include severe trauma (emergency life-threatening situations), broken bones, and controlling rejection of organ transplants.[39]

In contrast, neurologist Arthur Taub, who has taught at Yale University School of Medicine, calls acupuncture "nonsense with needles."[40] He visited Chinese hospitals that claimed to rely on acupuncture for anesthesia and reports that patients generally also received sedatives, narcotics, and/or local anesthesia before surgery.[41] Taub declares that acupuncture can expose patients to risks of nerve damage, and he worries that acupuncture could cause patients to forgo seeking conventional medical care for life-threatening diseases.[42] Other critics argue that acupuncture is nothing more than a powerful placebo.[43]

Part of the debate stems from a lack of consensus on how acupuncture works. Energy flows through the body cannot be seen or measured objectively. As an alternative explanation, some researchers suggest needling points may affect the nervous system by triggering the release of hormones or other chemicals.[44]

Compounding the debate are difficulties designing studies to test acupuncture's effectiveness. Conventional medical researchers prefer double-blind tests, where neither the test subjects nor the people administering treatment know who gets the real treatment. Even when acupuncturists use real points for some test subjects and fake points for others, however, they obviously know which is which. Might they subconsciously communicate

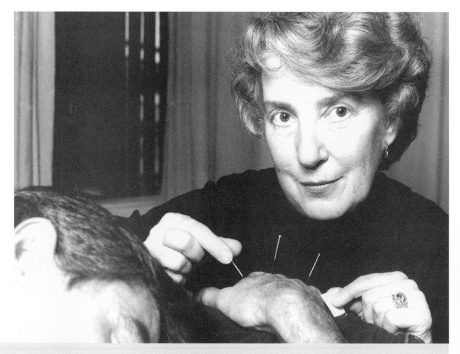

Associate Professor Carole Rogers demonstrates acupuncture to students at the UTS College of Acupuncture in Sydney, Australia.

greater expectations to patients receiving real treatment?[45]

Despite drawbacks, researchers are exploring whether acupuncture and its variations can help with specific problems.[46] In November 1997, a National Institutes of Health (NIH) panel announced that acupuncture can help control pain and nausea for certain illnesses.[47]

"The popular western view is that acupuncture is a placebo," says acupuncture professor Rogers, "but after twenty years of experience I find this is too glib an answer. The longer I practise the more I feel that the Chinese . . . knew a lot more about the subtle, energy aspects of human physiology than we do today."[48]

5

Herbal and Nutritional Therapies

What if you could grow medicine in your own backyard? Herbal medicine proponents say they bring a scientific perspective to folk remedies that can be at least as effective as expensive over-the-counter remedies.[1]

Herbal Medicine: More Than Folk Remedies?

Have a stomachache? Your great-grandparents might have suggested that you sip chamomile tea, suck on peppermint candy, or drink ginger ale. Botanist Douglas Schar explains that the

56

daisy plant known as German chamomile contains chemicals that counter the inflammation of stomach tissue and promote healing.[2] Oils in peppermint can help numb the stomach lining to burning stomach acid, stopping spasms that cause vomiting.[3] And ginger can increase gastric juice secretion to promote digestion.[4]

The supposed healing qualities of herbs cover a broad spectrum. Herbalists recommend rosemary to relieve headaches, improve circulation, stimulate

Herbal medicine advocates say ginger helps promote digestion.

Lemon balm is one of the many herbs used by practitioners of herbal and botanical medicine.

digestion, relieve depression, soothe painful menstrual periods, and even slow premature baldness or treat dandruff.[5] Lemon balm can be used for ailments ranging from colds and flu to headache, indigestion, and depression.[6] Uses for thyme include combating bronchitis and asthma, soothing muscle sprains, relieving headaches, soothing sore throats, and even treating childhood bed-wetting.[7]

Patients' perceptions of the healing power of herbs vary. Although Sara's mother has given her herbal medicines for ten years, Sara does not like it. "I don't like the capsules she gives me," says seventeen-year-old Sara. "They're really nasty." When high school pressures produced stress and depression, Sara's mom took her to her "herb lady," who recommended regular doses of Saint-John's-wort. "My mom said that I felt happier when I was taking it, but I couldn't tell any difference," says Sara. "It's sitting at home now, gathering dust."[8]

In contrast, Sara's thirteen-year-old sister, Mary, is a big fan of herbal treatments. "I think they work," she says. Mary had epileptic seizures when she was little. Drugs from her medical doctor weren't preventing seizures very effectively, so Mary's mom took her to an herbal consultant when she was seven years old. Mary doesn't recall all the herbs that were in the mixture, but she clearly remembers that she had only one or two seizures after she started taking herbal medicine. "I think it's helped," Mary says. "I haven't had any seizures in four years."[9]

Plant ingredients are found in many conventional medicines. Herbalists claim, however, that "natural" products are superior to synthetically produced medicines. Most claims about herbal medicine are unproven. But some studies seem promising.

One 1997 study in *JAMA—Journal of the American Medical Association* suggested that a specific extract prepared from the ginkgo biloba tree could improve the mental functioning of Alzheimer's disease patients.[10] Herbalists promote the plant as a circulatory system aid, and it may improve blood flow to the brain.

Garlic was once used to ward off vampires, but herbalists now claim that garlic lowers risks of cancer and helps prevent heart disease. While many claims remain speculative, recent studies suggest the plant may help patients with high cholesterol levels.[11]

Once used as a snakebite remedy by American Indian tribes, the purple coneflower, Echinacea, is now promoted by herbalists as an immune system enhancer that wards off symptoms of cold and flu.[12]

Garlic is one of the plants used by herbal practitioners that is getting a second look from practitioners of conventional medicine. Studies suggest that high cholesterol levels may be lowered with regular consumption of garlic.

While some German studies on standardized Echinacea products suggest the herb can reduce the severity of symptoms, concentrations in U.S. products vary, and there have been few clinical trials of Echinacea in the United States.[13]

"Natural" Doesn't Necessarily Mean "Safe"

To combat chronic fatigue, Ruth began taking chaparral, an herbal medicine made from a desert shrub. The last thing on her mind was that the natural remedy could poison her liver. Yet after taking chaparral for ten months, Ruth had hepatitis and needed an immediate liver transplant.[14]

Used in herbal medicine for ailments ranging from the common cold to venereal disease, chaparral appears to be the culprit behind at least fifteen cases of liver disease.[15] Other herbal remedies linked to adverse reactions include willow bark, yohimbe, comfrey, jin bu huan, lobelia, coltsfoot, and germander.[16]

Some practitioners and manuals provide precautions about using plant remedies.[17] But these warnings rarely appear on product labels, since herbs are generally sold as foods or supplements, instead of as medicines.[18]

The lack of uniform product standards and marketplace regulation led *Consumer Reports* magazine to characterize buying botanical medicines as "Herbal Roulette."[19] Medical school professor Victor Herbert worries about genuinely ill patients who don't recover because they "use these fraudulent or bogus treatments instead of cures and therapies that are proven to work."[20]

Then there's the problem of "herbal abuse." While vacationing in Florida during spring break, twenty-year-old Paul took eight pills containing Ephedra, a Chinese herb also known as ma huang. Sale of the pills was legal at the time, and Paul heard they could mimic the high users got from the street drug MDMA, also known as "ecstasy." Within hours after taking the pills, Paul died.[21]

Former FDA commissioner David Kessler has called some herbal products "nothing more than street drugs masquerading as diet supplements."[22] Ephedra, for example, contains a strong stimulant that the FDA has linked to dangerously high blood pressure and heart attacks. With ephedrine-based stimulants responsible for at least seventeen deaths, the FDA has issued formal warnings, and some states, including Florida, now ban or regulate products sold to produce "herbal highs."[23]

Aromatherapy

Does the nose know better? As a variation on herbal medicine, aromatherapy practitioners say scents from natural extracts can enhance moods and relieve common maladies. Using massage, room diffusion, soaking, and other application methods, clients inhale aromatic chemicals in plant extracts. Practitioners trace aromatherapy back as far as ancient Egypt and China. But modern aromatherapy began in the 1920s when a French perfumer, René-Maurice Gattefossé, burned his hand and thrust it into the nearest cool liquid—a bowl of lavender oil. To Gattefossé's surprise, the oil soothed his pain.[24] Aromatherapists today use lavender to treat burns, banish insomnia, relieve headache, improve digestion, soothe cold symptoms, and prevent fainting.[25]

A single essential oil can be used for many health conditions. Aromatherapists describe geranium as a "balancing" oil that can treat problems as diverse as frostbite, infertility, diabetes, blood disorders, and throat infections.[26] Rosemary is believed to be a strengthening, invigorating oil that can treat memory loss, headaches, coughs, flu, arthritis, and rheumatism.[27] Other oils are promoted by aromatherapists as inducing relaxation, fighting depression, or providing a sense of invigoration.[28]

Depending on the condition being treated, aromatherapists may recommend adding oils to a bath, massaging oils into the skin, or spreading the scent throughout a room with a mist spray, light-bulb ring, or steam diffuser. Oils should not be taken internally (eaten or drunk). To avoid skin irritations, almost all essential oils must be diluted with a "carrier" oil, such as sweet almond oil or wheat germ oil.[29]

Based on the lack of scientific evidence for aromatherapy, authors of the *University of California, Berkeley Wellness Letter* concluded, "Smells don't cure diseases."[30] Indeed, since oils have distinctive scents, it is especially hard to design double-blind

Aromatherapy uses essential oils extracted from plants to treat a variety of conditions. The essential oils pictured here are lavender, geranium, frankincense, chamomile, citronella, peppermint, ylang ylang, eucalyptus, sweet orange, tea tree, jasmine, and rosemary.

tests where neither subjects nor testers know who gets the placebo.

Having taught psychology for more than twenty years, skeptic Lynn McCutcheon suggests that claims about aromatherapy are flawed by "confused causation." Soaking in a warm bath with a few drops of lavender oil may be relaxing, says McCutcheon, but is it the lavender oil or the warm water that helps relieve stress?[31]

Despite the lack of scientific evidence, therapists, health product suppliers, and nationwide chains enjoy booming sales of aromatherapy products. Fifteen-year-old Laura's collection of oils includes lavender, geranium, rosemary, tangerine, and grapefruit essential oils, plus several carrier oils. "I don't know if they really work," says Laura, "but I use them because they smell good."[32]

The Macrobiotic Way

Practitioners of both conventional and alternative medicine agree that diet plays an important role in health. But the role of particular foods and nutritional supplements is hotly debated. Macrobiotics is just one of dozens of nutritional therapies. Japanese philosopher George Ohsawa first promoted macrobiotics in the late 1950s. The Kushi Institute and Foundation in Massachusetts has spearheaded the macrobiotic movement in the United States.[33]

Macrobiotic philosophy categorizes foods along a continuum ranging from extremely yin to very yang.[34] Foods at either end of the spectrum supposedly encourage the buildup of toxins and lead to disease. Examples of foods with "excess yin" include refined sugars, ice cream, chocolate, and processed foods. "Excess yang" foods are meat, eggs, cheese, and other animal products. Macrobiotics advocates say a balanced diet of foods in the middle of the continuum leads to good health.

Overall, a "standard" macrobiotic diet for preventing disease includes about 50 to 60 percent whole cereal grains, 5 percent soups, 20 to 25 percent vegetables, and 5 to 10 percent beans and sea vegetables. Brown rice is a staple of the macrobiotic diet, along with other whole grains. Beans, tofu, and round cabbage are also considered "balanced" foods. Permissible yin foods include high-fat seeds and nuts, large fruits, mustard greens, and Chinese cabbage, while yang foods include carrots, turnips, sea vegetables, and occasional servings of fish.[35]

Macrobiotics couples its dietary regimen with a positive outlook on life. The Kushi Institute maintains that macrobiotics is "more than brown rice": rather, it is a "way of life."[36]

While many diets aim to minimize the risk of disease, macrobiotics advocates say their therapy

Brown rice is a mainstay of a macrobiotic diet.

can actually promote a cure once disease sets in. Practitioners believe a personalized diet that counters the imbalance between yin and yang can help cure such serious diseases as epilepsy, pancreatic cancer, skin cancer, and prostate cancer.[37]

Advocates like Edward Esko insist macrobiotics is not offered "in place of" qualified medical care.[38] Yet some patients abandon conventional medical treatment.

Lenore was a Cincinnati chef who initially blessed macrobiotics for curing her asthma. Convinced she was better, Lenore gave up her inhalers. When a severe asthma attack followed, Lenore wound up in the hospital.[39]

Emily's doctor said she needed surgery to remove her right ovary and determine whether a tumor there was benign or cancerous. Instead, Emily decided to take her chances with macrobiotics. After she followed the diet religiously for six months, the tumor disappeared.[40]

Did the macrobiotic diet cure Emily, or did a noncancerous condition cure itself spontaneously? Medical doctor Stephen Barrett argues that no controlled scientific studies have proven that macrobiotics can actually cure disease.[41]

How does a macrobiotic practitioner determine what is out of balance? Diagnosis requires taking the pulse at surface and deep levels on each hand to gauge the state of internal organs. The face is also a storehouse of information for the macrobiotic practitioner. Theory holds that the nose shows the state of the heart and lungs, while the lips reflect the condition of the intestines and stomach. Different parts of the eyes are supposed to reflect the condition of internal organs.[42]

Dietitian and critic Jack Raso classifies these and other diagnostic tools as unscientific.[43] Moreover, claims Raso, the macrobiotic food plan is far from balanced and presents serious risks of iron, calcium, and vitamin deficiencies. He believes patients who want to reduce their risks of cancer, heart disease, obesity, and other diseases can follow other low-fat or vegetarian diets without running the risks presented by macrobiotics.[44]

Another concern is that the macrobiotic diet may dangerously restrict fluid intake.[45] In contrast, many nutrition experts urge people to drink eight glasses of water or other fluids daily.

Vitamin and Mineral Therapies

Vitamins are part of the daily routine for millions of men, women, and children. While multivitamin pills prevent specific deficiency diseases, advocates of supplement therapies claim they come nowhere near to realizing the curing potential of vitamins, minerals, enzymes, and other nutrients. With Americans spending more than $3 billion a year on nutritional supplements, many buyers obviously agree.[46]

Vitamin C is one of the most popular supplements. Besides potentially boosting the body's immune system, vitamin C is an antioxidant that can help neutralize free radicals—chemicals that may damage cells. Advocates like the late Linus Pauling believed vitamin C could help prevent cancer and other diseases. Some vitamin proponents recommend smaller amounts, but Pauling suggested doses of six grams per day for healthy people.[47]

Can vitamins cure disease? In one study of "hopeless" cancer cases, sixteen out of one hundred patients who received large doses of vitamin C survived for more than a year, as opposed to only three patients in a control group of one thousand who did not receive the megadoses.[48] Although its

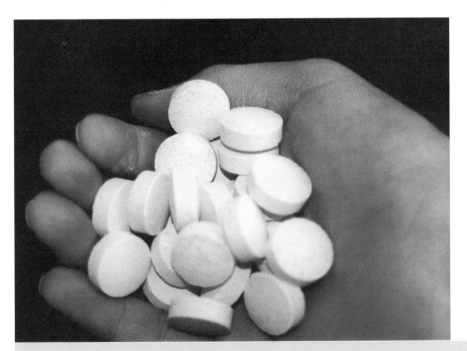

This photo shows six grams of vitamin C—the daily dose recommended by the late Linus Pauling. Vitamin C is a nutrient commonly found in citrus fruits, juices, and other foods.

effectiveness is unproven, vitamin C has also been used in alternative medicine therapies for mononucleosis, infertility, allergies, and even AIDS.

Other supplements used in alternative medicine therapies include vitamin A, calcium, thiamine, vitamin B6, vitamin E, zinc, beta carotene, niacin, iron, selenium, pantothenic and folic acids, enzymes, and even organ extracts. Some supplement therapies claim that nutrients boost the immune system, leading to better overall health and holding cancer at bay. Other therapies focus on preventing specific problems, such as heart disease.[49]

The Benefits of Supplements

Some studies suggest that supplements do provide health benefits. A review of studies on calcium supplements suggests the mineral reduces the risk of pregnancy-induced high blood pressure.[50] This is in addition to health data accepted by conventional medicine practitioners which show that dietary calcium reduces the risks of osteoporosis, a condition of brittle, easily broken bones.[51] Other studies suggest that vitamin E may help prevent or treat heart disease in nonsmokers.[52]

However, many claims are unproven. Boasts of better immunity and increased sexual prowess from zinc supplements have not been documented.[53]

Other studies read like a "good news, bad news" story. One study suggested that patients could reduce their chances of prostate, colon, and lung cancers with daily doses of selenium, a mineral found in certain grains, dairy products, organ meats, swordfish, tuna, and garlic.[54] The bad news, however, is that selenium overdoses can lead to hair loss, neurological problems, fingernail problems, liver damage, and respiratory failure.[55]

Indeed, megadoses of most vitamins and minerals can be dangerous, warns dietitian Kristine Napier. Overdoses of vitamin C present a risk of diarrhea, nausea, cramps, and headache. Too much vitamin A leads to liver damage, headaches, hair loss, and joint pain. Overdoses of zinc shrink red blood cells and impair immunity, which is the body's ability to fight off diseases.[56]

Dietitian Jack Raso argues that a balanced diet probably provides more health benefits than any vitamin and mineral therapies focused on isolated nutrients. He is especially critical when some companies selling mail-order supplements make unproven boasts that preparations maintain life, destroy toxins, strengthen the immune system, improve stamina and endurance, and provide effortless, guaranteed weight loss.[57]

6

Healing Hands

Have you ever had a back rub? How about a neck and shoulder massage? Most people say massages feel great. But is there such a thing as healing touch?

Among the dozens of touch and massage therapies in alternative medicine today are neuromuscular massage, deep tissue massage, Rosen Method, Hellerwork, Trager therapy, Alexander Technique, shiatsu, polarity therapy, and Reiki.

Some therapies claim to replace medical treatment. Others are complementary treatments that are used in addition to care by conventional doctors. This chapter examines three "healing hands" therapies.

Therapeutic Touch

As an experienced nurse, New York University nursing professor Dolores Krieger hated the frustration of caring for patients under circumstances in which she could not ease their pain. Nurses are not allowed to prescribe medication or order surgery. But they do touch patients while caring for them.

Intrigued by people who claimed to heal others by touch, Krieger wondered whether nurses and others could use this skill. Together with Dora Kunz, Krieger developed Therapeutic Touch in the 1970s. Today thousands of people, primarily nurses, practice Therapeutic Touch—often in conventional medical hospitals.

Like Ayurveda, homeopathy, and other alternative medicine systems, Therapeutic Touch presumes there is a universal life energy flowing through everyone. Krieger and her colleagues believed this energy extends beyond the patient. Moreover, they said, energy can be sensed and transferred from person to person.

While Therapeutic Touch does not depend on the patient's faith in the procedure, it requires the therapist to consciously become a "vehicle" for universal life energy. Before a typical session, the therapist prepares by mentally focusing on a tree, mountain, or another calming nature image. Once he or she feels at peace, treatment can begin.

The therapist gently massages the patient's neck and shoulders. Then the therapist moves his or her hands around the patient's body four to six inches away from the skin. Working with healthy people, therapists say they detect a balanced energy field as either a gentle vibration or a soft warmth evenly distributed around the body.

With an ill person, however, therapists perceive interruptions in the field. They sense these interruptions as heaviness, pressure, emptiness, coldness, pins and needles, static, and other feelings.

Focusing on the area of imbalance, the therapist wills energy to transfer from himself or herself to the patient. Often the therapist does this while holding his or her hand over the affected area. Other therapists may actually touch the patient during this part of the treatment.[1] Therapeutic Touch instructor and nurse Janet Macrae says the free flow of energy during treatment should not only help the patient but also leave the therapist feeling replenished.[2]

Afterward, patients rest quietly for twenty to thirty minutes. Some people report tingling or warmth during treatment; others report having no unusual sensations. Many say the sessions leave them feeling relaxed.[3]

Practitioners claim success in helping to heal broken bones, dealing with manic depression (a psychological disorder) in psychiatric patients, reducing fever and discomfort in AIDS patients, and calming patients with Alzheimer's or Parkinson's diseases.[4] A federally funded study at the University of Alabama at Birmingham Burn Center found patients treated with Therapeutic Touch showed a statistically significant improvement, although critics have challenged the study's methods and conclusions.[5]

Criticism of Therapeutic Touch

Critic Wallace Sampson, who has taught at Stanford University School of Medicine and served as board chairman of the National Council Against Health Fraud, says there is no objective evidence that energy is actually transferred from practitioner to patient in Therapeutic Touch. Instead, he believes psychological suggestion accounts for any patient improvements.[6]

David Sneed, an osteopathic doctor who practices family medicine, and his wife, Sharon Sneed, a dietitian, recognize that nurses want to help their patients, but they are skeptical about Therapeutic Touch. They criticize the technique's reliance on unseen life energy as being unscientific and superstitious. Additionally, they are suspicious about the necessity for the practitioner's meditative state, which they label an "altered state of consciousness."[7]

Other critics include Philadelphia registered nurses Robert Glickman and Janet Burns, who say they failed to sense any energy after attending a lecture on Therapeutic Touch and trying the technique.[8] Meanwhile, Therapeutic Touch is popular with many other nurses and patients, who use it as a supplement to conventional medicine.

Even if the therapy's effectiveness is never conclusively proven, practitioners believe they are helping patients feel better.[9]

Getting Back in Line

Like it or not, we can not "turn off" gravity on earth. But Ida Rolf (1896–1979) reasoned that bringing the body back into its natural alignment would help people function better with gravity.

Rolf earned her doctorate degree in biochemistry in 1920 from Columbia University's College of Physicians and Surgeons. She also studied chiropractic and yoga. While living in New York from the 1930s to the 1950s, she worked on developing her own form of physical manipulation therapy. In 1972, Rolf established the Rolf Institute of Structural Integration in Boulder, Colorado.[10]

Rolf called her therapy of surface and deep tissue massage "structural integration." Rolf described her technique as "rebuilding a sagging or bulging brick wall, rather than trying to prop it up by artificial means."[11] The bodywork treatment seeks to relieve chronic pain and stress and provide freer movement. Today the method is known as Rolfing.

In addition to addressing physical complaints, Rolf believed that psychological disorders could often be traced back to physical problems. For example, she used the hypothetical case of Johnny, whose alignment was upset when he fell down a flight of stairs at the age of ten. Since Johnny didn't feel right, he grew up feeling insecure, until at the

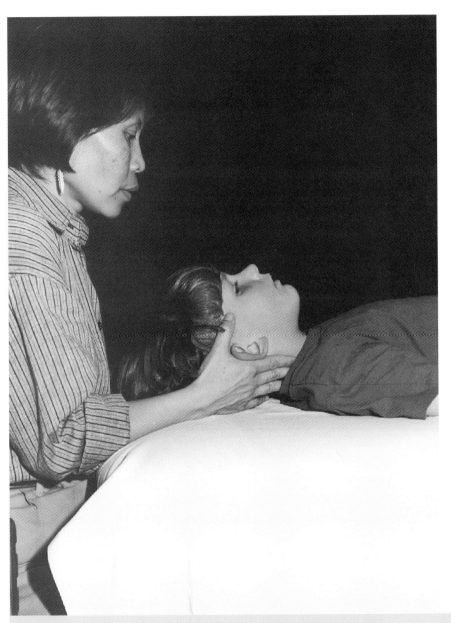

Rolfing practitioner Ashuan Seow works with a patient.

age of thirty-five he finally needed psychotherapy.[12] Based on this model, Rolf claimed her therapy could help patients with emotional conflicts. Today, the therapy is still used for some people in psychotherapy.[13]

Treatment usually consists of ten sessions. With forceful, probing movements, therapists work to loosen fascia, a term Rolf used for the flexible tissue surrounding and connecting muscles. The fascia is supposed to move easily, but practitioners say that both emotional trauma and physical injury can alter structure and restrict movement.

Typically, the first session would correct structure problems of the feet. Later sessions would work their way up the body to correct problems of the legs, pelvis, spine, shoulders, and head.[14]

Various patients report that treatments leave them feeling "alive," "tingling," "expansive," and "taller." Others say sessions can be painful, although Rolf claimed that any pain from treatment was a temporary sensation without lasting harmful effects. She distinguished between ongoing, chronic pain related to poor health and the discomfort occasionally reported during treatment, which she claimed was related to the dramatic changes accomplished by her technique.[15]

Jack Raso, a dietitian and critic of various alternative medicine therapies, reports that his fifteen-minute experience with the treatment was a pleasant experience, although he says his lower back felt sore later in the day. He suggests that other patients' sessions can sometimes be painful enough to be dangerous on a long-term basis. He also questions the notion that correcting physical structural imbalances can effectively treat psychological problems.[16]

Meanwhile, practitioners and patients using Rolf's method believe it lets the body work properly with the force of gravity. In turn, they say, the body is better able to cope with stresses and to heal itself.

A Firm Footing for Reflexology?

Reflexology—also called zone therapy—holds that ailments of different body organs can be cured by massaging the feet, hands, and other areas. Its use in the United States traces back to 1907, when William Fitzgerald taught that vertical zones of the body correspond to different areas of the foot. The toe end generally represents the head, and the heel corresponds roughly to lower parts of the body.

Reflexologists believe that energy channels between parts of the foot and different zones of the body can become blocked, hindering nerve impulses and interfering with the body's functions. Therapy seeks to remove those blockages and restore health.[17]

Without specifically promising to cure particular illnesses, various Internet articles note that reflexology has been used to treat a wide variety of health problems. These include stress, high blood pressure, back pain, asthma, constipation, arthritis, diabetes, and multiple sclerosis.[18]

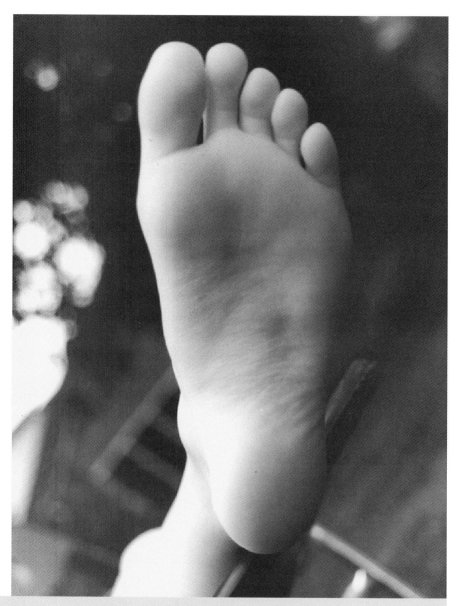

Reflexology maintains that massaging points on the foot can relieve stress and improve health.

In their book *Magic or Medicine?*, cancer specialist Robert Buckman and science writer Karl Sabbagh argue that reflexology has "little or no overlap" with conventional medicine. While many reflexologists and their clients claim sessions help relieve stress, critics note there is no objective evidence that organs like the liver or pancreas function better because of the treatments.[19]

Many patients using reflexology, Rolfing, and other massage techniques claim the therapies help. On the other hand, consider the views of Robert Carroll, who teaches philosophy at Sacramento City College and is the author of the on-line book *The Skeptic's Dictionary*:

> There is undoubtedly something to all this talk about trigger points, unblocked nerve endings, improved blood circulation and relief of pain. And the truth is, if I have to listen to you babble about balanced states and structural balance in order to get a massage, I'll do it. You might think you're enhancing my spiritual self-realization and bringing my life-force into harmony, structure and balance, but I'm just enjoying the massage.[20]

7

Mind Over Matter

Can pain and disease be willed away? Psychological factors—emotion, attitude, and stress—can cause illnesses whose symptoms and pain are very real. Turning the theory around, some alternative practitioners believe the power of the mind can also heal.

Taking Control?

Migraine headaches were a constant nightmare for ten-year-old Nicki. After drugs and other methods failed to provide relief, she went to a medical clinic at a university in Ohio.

82

Sitting very still, Nicki watched a design dance on a computer screen. Sensors connected to the machine measured her skin's electrical resistance. The more Nicki relaxed, the more the resistance diminished, and the more the screen's design shrank. Over time, Nicki learned to practice this relaxation pattern, using mental images of her favorite activities. Gradually, the frequency and severity of her migraines diminished.[1]

Using machines to help a patient control physical responses is part of the alternative therapy called biofeedback. Patients with conditions ranging from headaches to diabetes to high blood pressure try to consciously control responses that are often thought of as automatic.

One common technique involves training patients to warm their hands and feet by using mental images, such as sitting around a campfire. As machines provide objective measurements of skin temperature, patients receive reinforcement for their efforts. They learn what "works" and what does not.

One survey of fifty-four high-blood-pressure patients by the Menninger Foundation found that after learning biofeedback, 93 percent were able to eliminate or reduce their medications.[2] Still, the number of large, controlled studies remains small.

Most practitioners are trained psychologists, although some individuals practicing biofeedback lack such training. Psychiatrist and consumer advocate Stephen Barrett also questions whether many patients might have learned the same relaxation skills by using methods other than biofeedback.[3]

Stress reduction is also a goal of mind-over-matter alternative medicine therapies. By learning meditation techniques, breathing exercises, and other therapies, patients seek to release tension and, it is hoped, promote healing.

Jon Kabat-Zinn, who has directed a chronic pain clinic at the University of Massachusetts Medical Center, admits many patients are skeptical and "not at all interested" in Zen masters or gurus.[4] Yet he says the clinic often helps patients "work around the edges" and cope with their pain.[5]

Kabat-Zinn and other proponents of stress-reduction therapies admit the evidence is not conclusive. Nonetheless, they say, the therapy might provide real benefits in "symptom reduction"—a decrease in the number and frequency of physical and psychological symptoms reported by patients.[6]

Imagery

Can you imagine yourself better? That is the goal of imagery and visualization therapies.

If acne is a problem, you might imagine yourself standing in an open field, stretching toward the sun and absorbing sun rays through small hands and eyes at the ends of your fingertips. Then, with a golden brush in one of the imaginary sunbeam hands, you would scrub your acne. Another imaginary sunbeam hand would shine a blue laser

Patients practicing relaxation therapies may imagine calming nature scenes.

light on the area, and a third sunbeam hand could apply a salve of sunshine and blue sky.

Psychiatrist Gerald Epstein recommends doing such a visualization in cycles of three weeks on and one week off.[7] Does the mental imagery really help clear up acne, or would many acne flare-ups pass anyway after several weeks?

Mental imagery is also used as a complementary or add-on therapy for more serious diseases. Nine-year-old Jason was an avid *Star Trek* fan. While doctors used conventional medical therapies to treat Jason's cancer, counselors encouraged the boy to visualize himself as a space fleet commander.

Imagining that his disease-fighting white blood cells were lasers and torpedoes, Jason mentally "bombed" his tumors.

Despite setbacks, Jason persisted with his imagery. Eventually, the boy recovered. While admitting that the conventional therapies had been helpful, Jason believed the imagery was the primary reason for his cure.[8] In other words, rather than viewing the imagery as an add-on to conventional treatment, Jason felt the imagery itself was the real cure.

Retired surgeon Bernie Siegel, whose books include *Love, Medicine, and Miracles*, promotes imagery as a way for patients to take an active role in their cure. Siegel emphasizes that a loving and encouraging environment can help patients maximize the mind-body connection between their health and emotions. Instead of despairing, the patients feel hope.[9]

But many patients do not survive life-threatening diseases. As a health instructor at a major urban hospital, Carmen felt guilty about not finding the cancerous lump in her breast earlier. She underwent surgery, chemotherapy, and radiation. She also earnestly practiced imagery, visualizing herself commanding her body's defense mechanisms to attack and destroy the cancer. When Carmen died, she left behind a husband and two preschool children.[10]

Visualization did not cure Carmen's cancer, but did it help her deal better with the emotional trauma of being sick? Regardless of outcome, did it help her to take an active role in her treatment? Carmen's husband would like to think so.

But might imagery therapy have amplified Carmen's feelings of guilt when the cancer continued to spread? Does telling a patient she is personally responsible for her survival imply that, if she isn't cured, it must be because she didn't try hard enough? These are among the questions raised by cancer specialist Robert Buckman and science writer Karl Sabbagh.[11]

Critics David and Sharon Sneed argue that a "think-yourself-well" mentality can cause emotional harm by making patients deny the severity of their health problem. Moreover, they argue that imagery, meditation, and other therapies that rely upon "altered states" of consciousness are inherently suspect. They suggest that such therapies can leave patients vulnerable to psychological harm from having their minds improperly "manipulated."[12]

Positive Comments on Guided Imagery

Despite criticisms, psychotherapists such as Belleruth Naparstek say patients' positive comments show that they get real benefits from guided imagery. Naparstek's audiotapes describe imagery sessions for patients with cancer, organ transplants, high blood pressure, asthma, multiple sclerosis, and other diseases. She also says that imagery can strengthen the immune system and help with minor discomforts like insomnia or allergies.[13]

For example, Naparstek recommends an exercise

for "cellular imagery" that guides patients to place one hand over the thymus (just below the collarbone) and another over the belly. In the fourteen-minute exercise, patients imagine "a soft, healing warmth" coming out of their hands, entering the body, and penetrating deep into the glands to stimulate and revitalize the immune cells. Patients visualize their immune cells as "miraculous little soldier cells," ready to defend the body from any and all attacks.[14]

Does this or similar exercises provide tangible benefits for general health maintenance? Or does it really matter as long as patients feel they are doing something positive for their health? The jury is still out.

A Matter of Faith?

For fourteen years, Vince and Debbie had been loyal members of an Indiana-based church called the Faith Assembly. Church members do not use conventional medical treatments. They sincerely believe God will provide both spiritual and physical healing for their families.

When the couple's twenty-three-month-old daughter, Jessica, became ill, the family prayed instead of taking her to a medical doctor. At first, Jessica seemed to improve, but then her condition grew worse. Within four days, Jessica died from bronchitis and bronchial pneumonia. "We did not expect her death at all," Debbie mourned.

Jessica's death was a tragedy, but Vince and Debbie's nightmares were not over. The couple was arrested and charged with reckless child endangerment. At the trial in Mercer County, Ohio, three doctors testified that Jessica could have survived with medical treatment, including prescription antibiotics. "Their trust in the Lord cost [their daughter] her life," the prosecutor said.[15]

Members of the Church of Christ, Scientist,[16] the Faith Assembly, and certain other groups believe that faith alone can cure them of disease. To the extent adults make decisions about their own health care, the First Amendment to the United States Constitution guarantees freedom of religion.

But lawmakers in most states believe it is inexcusable for parents to deny children necessary medical care. They have enacted laws mandating immunizations before children attend school and requiring parents to obtain emergency medical care for life-threatening conditions.[17]

Aside from organized religions that avoid conventional treatments, charismatic faith healers loudly call on God to cure members of their congregations. One "healing" evangelist would shout out names of people in the audience and tell about their ailments. While he claimed God gave him the information, in actuality his wife collected facts from staff members who mingled with the audience. She then transmitted the information to a radio receiver hidden in her husband's ear.[18]

Other faith healers may be honest individuals who sincerely believe in what they are doing. But critics like psychiatrist Stephen Barrett and

Episcopal journalist Reverend Lester Kinsolving say that, at most, faith healers spark only a placebo response. Caught up in the excitement of the prayer meeting, patients may temporarily perceive that pain is lessened. Moreover, critics say, even honest practitioners rarely have the basic training needed to recognize situations that require immediate treatment from conventional medical doctors.[19]

The weight of opinion seems to be that few, if any, faith healers can accomplish miracles on demand. Whether miracles sometimes occur is a different question. By definition, faith is belief in something that cannot be scientifically proved or disproved.

Does Prayer Make a Difference?

"I'm sorry your dad's in the hospital," says Jill. "I'll say a prayer for him." Even if you wouldn't say this to a friend, you probably know people who would. When Harvard medical professor David Eisenberg and his colleagues surveyed people about the use of alternative medicine about 25 percent said they pray regularly.[20]

Most of those people probably view prayer as a supplement to conventional medical treatment rather than as a substitute. They ask God for success of the medical treatment. If the treatment is not successful, they ask God for grace for themselves and their families.

One study at San Francisco General Hospital had members of Christian groups pray daily for the recovery of certain patients in the coronary care unit. Neither patients, doctors, nor nurses knew who was prayed for and who was not. At the end of ten months, patients who had been prayed for were less likely to need antibiotics, less likely to require tubes for assisted breathing, and less likely to develop fluid in the lungs.[21] Were the prayers being answered, or could the results have occurred by chance?

Devoutly religious people acknowledge that sometimes prayers are answered the way people hope and sometimes they are not. Pamela was forty-nine years old when her monthly breast exam turned up a lump. When doctors first told her it was cancerous, she was devastated. She underwent surgery, hormone treatments, chemotherapy, and radiation therapy. She and her family also prayed.

As more people learned about Pamela's situation, they prayed too—not just in Pamela's church but at the school where Pamela taught computer science, the hospital where her husband worked, other churches where friends went, prayer groups in the town where a daughter went to college, and even a Christian bookstore where Pamela didn't know anybody.

"I can't say for sure if it's made a difference in whether I'll be cured," Pamela says, "but it's definitely made a difference in the quality of my life. Knowing that all these people are praying for me means so much. It's given me a sense of peace that I never would have felt otherwise."[22]

8

Making Decisions

By looking at selected branches of
alternative medicine, this book gives you
an idea of some of the claims and
controversies surrounding these treatments. The description of each method is
an overview, and there are many nuances
in both theory and practice. Additionally,
there are dozens more therapies that come
under the heading of alternative medicine.

Scratching the Surface

Some remedies target particular diseases,
such as cancer, arthritis, or heart disease.
Others aim generally to boost the immune

system, hoping to help the body fight off disease naturally.

Some treatments promote specific foods or medicines, such as shark cartilage or bee products. Others rely on physical forces, such as heat, cold, or water therapies. Still other branches of alternative medicine use psychological cues, such as music, to tap into stress reduction, relaxation, and healing.

Then there is naturopathy. Naturopathic physicians believe that natural remedies boost the body's inherent ability to heal itself. After four years of special training that includes advanced biology and other medical subjects, practitioners select and combine different natural remedies from acupuncture, nutrition supplements, homeopathy, chiropractic, and other disciplines.[1]

For every branch of alternative medicine, you can be sure there are advocates who say the discipline promises substantial health benefits. And you can be just as sure that there are critics who challenge it and demand scientific proof.

Even advocates of conventional medicine will quickly admit that it does not have all the answers to the medical problems facing the world's population. But are there areas where alternative medicine can serve patients better than conventional medicine?

Recognizing that Western medicine may not have all the answers, the National Institutes of Health (NIH) formed the Office of Alternative Medicine (OAM) in 1991. By funding grants for research, the office wants to know whether scientific proof can be developed for different treatment methods.[2]

Since then, OAM has provided limited funding for peer-reviewed studies on the effectiveness of alternative therapies in specific contexts. For example, rather than considering the effectiveness of acupuncture in general, one study compares the relative success of acupuncture versus a common drug to treat ADHD (attention deficit hyperactivity disorder).[3]

However, the vast bulk of government research funding still goes for studies in conventional medicine. As of March 1997, OAM's annual budget was $12 million—a "paltry" amount, according to Democratic Representative Peter DeFazio of Oregon. "We know from surveys that one-third of Americans use 'alternative' techniques," said DeFazio, "but the current office isn't even a blip on the radar screen of NIH."[4]

"Alternative medicine doesn't replace conventional medicine," says Wayne Jonas, who has served as OAM director. "But it can fill in where traditional treatments require supplement."[5] A 1996 survey by the Association of American Medical Colleges found that 92 out of 125 medical schools in the United States, including Harvard Medical School, now offer courses in one or more therapies used in alternative medicine.[6]

No single study will settle once and for all whether a particular therapy is valid. However, research may find instances where alternative medicine may be a less expensive, yet more effective, choice for treating certain conditions. Or research may show that using some therapies together with biomedicine increases chances for a speedy recovery. As more studies are critically reviewed within the scientific community, health care providers will understand better the promises and limitations of alternative medicine.

Desperate Measures

While studies continue, sick people are often desperate to find something—anything—that offers any hope for a cure. Generally, however, medicines can be prescribed as cures in the United States only if the FDA agrees they have been proven safe and effective for the intended use. But agency review takes time that many sick people just do not have. Should a dying patient be at the mercy of a government agency when it comes to getting what might possibly be a life-saving medicine?

The FDA is aware that people want potential new cures to be reviewed swiftly, but the agency does not want to shortchange public safety just to save time. Many drugs proposed as possible treatments for cancer, AIDS, and other serious diseases fail to meet standards for government approval.

Derived from apricot pits, laetrile was promoted as a possible cure for cancer as early as the 1950s. Studies at the Mayo Clinic and elsewhere in the 1980s produced no evidence that it was effective in treating cancer. As of 1997, the drug had never been approved by the FDA.[7]

Critics like psychiatrist and consumer advocate Stephen Barrett argue that patients using unproven remedies like laetrile are being duped by "cancer quackery." They question whether consent to unproven remedies can ever be truly informed when people are desperate for survival.[8]

Yet people still travel to Mexico to purchase laetrile, hoping the medicine will help treat cancer, AIDS, or other diseases. After one professional baseball outfielder had surgery and radiation treatments for a rare form of tonsil cancer, he used laetrile purchased in Tijuana, Mexico. He also took huge daily doses of vitamins and adopted a low-fat diet with no red meat or coffee. "It's our responsibility as individuals to go out and find what the cure is," the player told *USA Today Baseball Weekly* as his recovery was under way.[9]

Caustic Cons

As discussed in earlier chapters, there is a vigorous debate going on about whether alternative therapies have scientific and medical value. Advocates call the treatments cures. Critics label them quackery.

Beyond this, both alternative and conventional medicine are plagued by another problem: fraud. While most health care providers are honest and well-meaning, a small segment schemes to profit from patients' gullibility, fear, and insecurity.

One California medical doctor and his partner

called their treatment "Immunostim." Patients with cancer and AIDS paid up to $7,500 for each painful injection, and the partners raked in more than $670,000 for their "treatment." Then FDA laboratory analysis showed the "medicine" contained chemicals commonly found in dishwasher detergent and toilet bowl cleaner.

When criminal charges were filed, the defendants argued their treatment was "alternative medicine." But the judge said it was "snake oil." Both the doctor and his partner were convicted in 1995, and the Medical Board of California revoked the doctor's license. By then, more than half the patients had died from their ailments.[10]

In Twin Falls, Idaho, an alternative medicine practitioner offered patients a variety of natural cures. On the side, he sold mail-order immunization kits that promised to protect children from polio, scarlet fever, smallpox, measles, typhoid, tetanus, whooping cough, mumps, and diphtheria. But the FDA claimed that buyers got only water and alcohol solutions and sugar pills, and the agency urged parents to obtain standard immunizations for their children.[11] Did parents understand that they were buying homeopathic medications, or were they misled into believing that they were buying vaccines that had been clinically proven to be as effective as shots given by conventional medical doctors?

One FDA estimate put the out-of-pocket cost to Americans from health fraud at $30 billion a year. Beyond this, there are hidden costs. Some patients are hurt by fraudulent treatments themselves. Others forgo conventional treatment that could have saved their lives.[12]

Although teenagers are a comparatively healthy segment of the population, they are a prime target of health-fraud promoters. Robert Carroll, author of the on-line book *The Skeptic's Dictionary*, says, "I would advise teens to be wary of appeals to their vanity in place of evidence."[13]

Heading this category are plans to lose weight effortlessly without sensible dieting and exercise.[14] Ads also feed on teens' insecurity and concerns about peer pressure. Some of the more blatant scams include muscle-building pills, breast developers, and even skin creams promising to prevent transmission of herpes and HIV.[15]

Learn the warning signs of scams. First of all, if it sounds too good to be true, it probably is. This general consumer warning applies doubly to health fraud.

Be wary of claims that promise "amazing" or "miraculous" cures. Watch out for "guarantees" of improved memory, greater vigor, or instant results. No reputable health care provider can keep incredible promises of perfect health and invincibility.

Read the small print. While boldface print urges you to call a toll-free number right away, a tiny disclaimer may contradict the clear message of the ad by saying "no medical claims are made or implied."[16]

The FDA warns consumers to beware of testimonials from "satisfied customers." People touting the product may not even be real customers. They almost certainly did not take part in any controlled scientific study.

Any claim that doctors are "butchers" or that the medical community is persecuting the promoter is another warning sign. Learn to evaluate the source of information. Today's medical discoveries will be reported in headline news and peer-reviewed journals rather than in back-page ads of magazines.

Also be wary about offers of computer-scored questionnaires to diagnose "nutrient deficiencies." "Computers used for such tests are programmed to recommend supplements for virtually everyone, regardless of their symptoms or medical condition," says an FDA bulletin.[17]

If you suspect fraud, do not suffer in silence. Contact a government agency responsible for investigating fraud claims, such as your state attorney general's office, the FDA, the Federal Trade Commission, or the U.S. Postal Service (for mail-order products). Only by speaking up can you keep others from being victimized by con artists masquerading as healers.

What about You?

Whether you are undergoing conventional treatment or looking into an alternative therapy, do all you can to become an educated consumer. This book introduces you to several types of therapies and tells you the views of advocates and opponents of each treatment. Read further and find out more.

Keep in mind that most books and articles have a definite slant—either in favor of or against alternative medicine. Knowing this slant helps you to evaluate what the author says. Read and compare views from both sides.

Talk to people. Robert Carroll especially urges teens to "seek advice from someone who will not be likely to simply reinforce their wishes, but who will advise them on the basis of experience and knowledge."

If research makes you think that an alternative therapy might help you, try to find people who have used that therapy. How long have they been under treatment? What results have they had? What good and bad things do they have to say about their practitioner?

Before undergoing diagnosis and treatment, talk carefully with practitioners. Find out details about their education, licensing, and experience. Ask about their philosophy for treatment. Find out what types of problems they feel competent to handle and what circumstances they feel are best handled by medical doctors.

Do not be afraid to ask challenging questions. Has this treatment been studied in double-blind testing? What precautions should you take? Are there potential side effects? Will the practitioner share results of tests and treatment with your family physician?

Insist on getting answers to all your questions.

Do not give up until you understand the responses clearly enough to explain them to someone else.

Last, but not least, talk to your medical doctor about your choice of health treatments. When David Eisenberg and his colleagues surveyed Americans about their use of alternative medicine, he was shocked by the high percentage of patients who failed to inform their doctor about the alternative therapy.[18]

Your doctor can advise if there are precautions you should take when undergoing a particular alternative therapy, such as limits on full-body X rays, avoiding potentially toxic enema ingredients, and so forth. Besides sharing whatever information he or she may have about the therapy, your doctor can help make sure that you are not forgoing necessary immediate care if your problem turns out to be a serious or life-threatening illness.

It will be a long time until scientific research resolves all the debates surrounding alternative medicine. Until then, we all need to be questioning, informed consumers. After all, our health is at stake.

Glossary

acupuncture—An alternative medical therapy in which practitioners use needles to control the flow of energy, called *chi*, throughout the body.

advocate—A person who argues for a particular cause; another word for advocate is *proponent*.

alternative medicine—Treatment intended to address and improve a health condition that is not generally taught in United States medical schools and is not accepted by most medical doctors as supported by scientific documentation of safety and effectiveness.

aromatherapy—A type of herbal medicine that holds that scents from natural plant substances can promote health and healing.

Ayurveda—Traditional Indian medicine, which claims that imbalances in three forces or humors, called doshas, can lead to the buildup of toxins and cause disease.

biofeedback—A type of mind-body therapy in which patients get readings, or feedback, from machines and use the information to try to control body functions.

biomedicine—Also called *conventional medicine* or *allopathic medicine*, this is the style of medicine generally taught in United States medical schools and practiced by most medical and osteopathic doctors.

cancer—A life-threatening disease in which cells of one or more organs multiply abnormally as malignant tumors.

chiropractic—A branch of alternative medicine in which practitioners work to relieve pain and promote the body's ability to heal itself through adjustments (manipulating bones of the back) and related manual techniques.

complementary—Term used to describe alternative medicine therapies that are used in addition to, rather than instead of, conventional medical treatments.

control group—People in a study who do not receive active drugs or treatment.

critic—A person who questions and challenges a particular position.

double-blind test—A study where neither the test subjects nor the people administering treatment know whether someone is receiving the real treatment or an ineffective substitute, or *placebo*.

fraud—Deliberate deception of a person by selling a product or service that does not perform as promised.

herbal medicine—Also called *botanical medicine*, an alternative therapy that uses plant substances to treat illness and promote health.

holism—A medical approach that seeks to treat an individual as a whole person rather than as the sum of individual cells, organs, and body systems; holistic practitioners generally search for an underlying cause of disease instead of just treating symptoms.

homeopathy—A branch of alternative medicine based on the theory that dilute concentrations of substances that would otherwise produce symptoms similar to those of a disease can trigger the body's ability to heal itself.

imagery—A type of mind-body alternative medicine in which patients use mental images in an effort to promote healing.

macrobiotics—A nutritional diet centered around whole grains and fresh vegetables that seeks a particular balance between foods categorized as *yin* and *yang*.

mysticism—A belief in magic or supernatural forces.

placebo effect—Improvement in health linked to expectations that a treatment—even one without active ingredients—will produce a positive effect.

post hoc rationalization—Reasoning that if a patient got better after a particular therapy, it was the therapy, not other factors, that led to the improvement.

quackery—Practices of a person who pretends to (but does not) have medical skill to cure diseases.

reflexology—Also called *zone therapy*, a type of massage that uses points on feet, hands, or other body parts to attempt to stimulate healing.

Rolfing—A technique of bodywork massage intended to restore the body to its natural alignment and thereby treat physical and emotional problems.

Therapeutic Touch—An alternative therapy that claims to transfer universal life energy from practitioner to patient to aid healing.

toxic—Poisonous.

vitamins—A group of chemicals that, in small quantities, are necessary to prevent specific diseases; some alternative therapies urge taking large amounts, called *megadoses*, to prevent or cure disease.

Further Reading

"Alternative Medicine: The Facts," *Consumer Reports*, vol. 59, January 1994.

Barrett, Stephen, and William T. Jarvis, eds. *The Health Robbers: A Close Look at Quackery in America*. Buffalo: Prometheus Books, 1993.

Buckman, Robert, and Karl Sabbagh. *Magic or Medicine? An Investigation of Healing and Healers*. Amherst, N.Y.: Prometheus Books, 1995.

Butler, Kurt. *A Consumer's Guide to "Alternative Medicine."* Buffalo: Prometheus Books, 1992.

Castleman, Michael. *Nature's Cures*. Emmaus, Pa.: Rodale Books, 1996.

Collinge, William. *The American Holistic Health Association Complete Guide to Alternative Medicine*. New York: Warner Books, 1996.

Jacobs, Jennifer, ed. *The Encyclopedia of Alternative Medicine*. Boston: Journey Editions, 1996.

Janiger, Oscar, and Philip Goldberg. *A Different Kind of Healing: Doctors Speak Candidly about Their Successes with Alternative Medicine*. New York: Jeremy P. Tarcher/Putnam Books, 1993.

Nash, Barbara. *From Acupressure to Zen: An Encyclopedia of Natural Therapies*. Alameda, Calif.: Hunter House, 1996.

Raso, Jack. *"Alternative" Healthcare: A Comprehensive Guide.* Amherst, N.Y.: Prometheus Books, 1994.

Sinclair, Brett Jason. *Alternative Health Care Resources: A Directory and Guide.* West Nyack, N.Y.: Parker Publishing Company, 1992.

Stehlin, Isadora B. "An FDA Guide to Choosing Medical Treatments." *FDA Consumer,* vol. 29, June 1995, p. 10.

Chapter Notes

Chapter 1. In Search of a Better Way

1. Patient stories in this book are about actual persons, but all patient names have been changed to respect individuals' privacy.

2. Anthony J. Satillaro and Tom Monte, *Recalled by Life* (Boston: Houghton Mifflin Company, 1982), pp. 1–14, 41.

3. Ibid., pp. 54–55.

4. Ibid., pp. 149–152; Albert Marchetti, *Beating the Odds: Alternative Treatments That Have Worked Miracles against Cancer* (Chicago: Contemporary Books, 1988), pp. 91–94.

5. Jack Raso, *Mystical Diets: Paranormal, Spiritual, and Occult Nutrition Practices* (Buffalo: Prometheus Books, 1993), p. 24.

6. Oscar Janiger and Philip Goldberg, *A Different Kind of Healing: Doctors Speak Candidly about Their Successes with Alternative Medicine* (New York: Jeremy P. Tarcher/Putnam Books, 1993), p. 159.

7. Jack Raso, *"Alternative" Healthcare: A Comprehensive Guide* (Buffalo: Prometheus Books, 1994), pp. 44–45.

8. David M. Eisenberg et al., "Unconventional Medicine in the United States—Prevalence, Costs, and Patterns of Use," *New England Journal of Medicine*, vol. 328, January 28, 1993, p. 246.

9. Isadora Stehlin, "An FDA Guide to Choosing Medical Treatments," *FDA Consumer*, vol. 29, June 1995, p. 10.

Chapter 2. Conventional versus Alternative Medicine

1. *Alternative Medicine: Expanding Medical Horizons. Report to the National Institutes of Health* (Washington, D.C.: Government Printing Office, 1994), pp. xxxvii–xxxix.

2. Steve Parker, *Medicine* (New York: Dorling Kindersley, 1995), p. 16; Robert Buckman and Karl Sabbagh, *Magic or Medicine? An Investigation of Healing and Healers* (Amherst, N.Y.: Prometheus Books, 1995), pp. 16–22.

3 Susan Neiberg Terkel, *Colonial American Medicine* (New York: Franklin Watts, 1993), pp. 12–14; Buckman and Sabbagh, pp. 21–24.

4. David Ritchie and Fred Israel, *Health & Medicine* (New York: Chelsea House, 1995), pp. 22–24, 48–63.

5. *Alternative Medicine*, pp. xxxvii–xxxviii.

6. Founded in 1874 by Andrew Taylor Still, osteopathy started out as an "alternative" therapy, but osteopathic colleges adapted their schools to meet the Flexner standards. See, generally, Stephen Sandler, *Osteopathy: The Illustrated Guide* (New York: Harmony Books, 1989).

7. The viruses may still exist in laboratories but do not exist in the general population.

8. Anita Manning, "Vaccines Save Many Lives, But Cost Could Become Obstacle," *USA Today*, September 26, 1996, p. 3D.

9. Ann Giudici Fettner, "Low Back Pain: If It Ain't Broke . . . ," *Harvard Health Letter*, vol. 20, May 1995, p. 6.

10. T. Bonnett, *Confessions of a Healer: The Truth from an Unconventional Family Doctor* (Aspen, Colo.: MacMurray & Beck, 1994), pp. 18–21.

11. Buckman and Sabbagh, pp. 186–202.

12. Ibid., pp. 154–167.

Chapter 3. Homeopathy and Chiropractic

1. Compare Sarah Richardson, *Homeopathy: The Illustrated Guide* (New York: Harmony Books, 1988), pp. 15–19, 32–35, 124–129, with "Homeopathy: Much Ado About Nothing?" *Consumer Reports*, vol. 59, March 1994, p. 201.

2. Isadora Stehlin, "Homeopathy: Real Medicine or Empty Promises?" *FDA Consumer*, vol. 30, December 1996, p. 15. Richardson, pp. 46–52.

3. Michael Castleman, *Nature's Cures* (Emmaus, Pa.: Rodale Books, 1996), pp. 240–242.

4. Christopher Hammond, *The Complete Family Guide to Homeopathy* (New York: Penguin Studio, 1995), pp. 123–125.

5. "Homeopathy: Much Ado About Nothing?" (*Consumer Reports*), p. 201.

6. Quoted in Castleman, p. 239. See also Leah R. Garnett, "Homeopathy: Is Less Really More?" *Harvard Health Letter*, vol. 20, May 1995, pp. 1, 3.

7. Richardson, pp. 52–56.

8. Garnett, p. 3.

9. Ibid.; Stehlin, p. 19.

10. Stehlin, p. 19, referencing Jacobs's study and noting that an article in a subsequent issue of *Pediatrics* criticized her methodology.

11. Robert Buckman and Karl Sabbagh, *Magic or Medicine? An Investigation of Healing and Healers* (Amherst, N.Y.: Prometheus Books, 1995), pp. 195–197.

12. Compare Klaus Linde et al., "Are the Clinical Effects of Homeopathy Placebo Effects?" *Lancet*, vol. 350, Sept. 20, 1997, p. 834, with Jan Vandenbroucke, "Homeopathy Trials: Going Nowhere," *Lancet*, vol. 350, Sept. 20, 1997, p. 824; M. J. S. Langman, "Homeopathy Trials: Reason for Good Ones But Are They Warranted?" *Lancet*, vol. 350, Sept. 20, 1997, p. 825.

13. Garnett, p. 3.

14. Stehlin, p. 19, citing 1995 sales of $201 million.

15. Ibid.

16. David M. Eisenberg et al., "Unconventional Medicine in the United States—Prevalence, Costs, and Patterns of Use," *New England Journal of Medicine*, vol. 328, January 28, 1993, p. 246.

17. Glenn S. Rothfeld and Suzanne LeVert, *Natural Medicine for Back Pain: The Best Alternative Methods for Banishing Backache* (New York: St. Martin's Press for Rodale Press, 1996), pp. 117–118.

18. Nathaniel Altman, *Everybody's Guide to Chiropractic Health Care* (Los Angeles: Jeremy P. Tarcher, 1990), p. 59, quoting D. D. Palmer's account from *The Science, Art and Philosophy of Chiropractic*.

19. Terry A. Rondberg, *Chiropractic First: The Fastest Growing Healthcare Choice before Drugs or Surgery* (Chandler, Ariz.: Chiropractic Journal, 1996), pp. 10–12; Altman, p. 60, quoting D. D. Palmer.

20. George Magner, *Chiropractic: The Victim's Perspective* (Amherst, N.Y.: Prometheus Books, 1995), pp. 10–15.

21. Ibid., p. 14; Altman, p. 63.

22. Altman, pp. 64–67, 222; Rondberg, pp. 12–19; Magner, pp. 15–17.

23. Altman, pp. 68–70; Magner, pp. 18–20.

24. 671 F. Supp. 1465 (N.D. Ill., 1987), affirmed on appeal, discussed in Magner, pp. 138–141.

25. Compare Rondberg, pp. 115–117, and Altman, pp. 71–74, with Magner, pp. 137–142, and Kurt Butler, *A Consumer's Guide to "Alternative Medicine"* (Buffalo: Prometheus Books, 1992), pp. 72–74.

26. Butler, p. 90.

27. Rothfeld and LeVert, p. 117.

28. Ann Giudici Fettner, "Low Back Pain: If It Ain't Broke . . . ," *Harvard Health Letter*, vol. 20, May 1995, p. 6.

29. Altman, p. 139.

30. Magner, pp. 143–154; "Media Misleads Americans on Government Report and the Value of Chiropractors for Treating Back Pain," *NCAHF Newsletter*, vol. 18, May–June 1995, p. 1.

31. Magner, pp. 71–80.

32. "Chiropractors," *Consumer Reports*, vol. 59, June 1994, p. 383. See also Magner, pp. 187–188.

33. Debra Levinson, "The Benefits of Chiropractic during Pregnancy," *Special Delivery*, vol. 17, Fall 1994, p. 4.

34. Magner, pp. 163–165.

35. Ibid., pp. 4–8.

36. Ibid., pp. 165–176. See also "Chiropractors," *Consumer Reports*.

37. Altman, pp. 143–145.

38. Ibid., pp. 125–126; Rondberg, p. 56; Rothfeld and LeVert, p. 120.

39. Compare Rondberg, pp. 81–88, with Stephen Barrett and William T. Jarvis, eds., *The Health Robbers* (Buffalo: Prometheus Books, 1993), pp. 171–175.

40. Shelly Downing, "A Tale of Two Remedies," *American Fitness*, vol. 12, November–December 1994, p. 38.

Chapter 4. Alternative Medicine from India and China

1. Gopi Warrier and Deepika Gunawant, *The Complete Illustrated Guide to Ayurveda* (Rockport, Mass.: Element Books, 1997), pp. 37–55.

2. Vasant Lad, *Ayurveda: The Science of Self-Healing*, 2nd ed. (Wilmot, Wis.: Lotus Press, 1985), pp. 26–31; Vinod Verma, *Ayurveda: A Way of Life* (York Beach, Maine: Samuel Weiser, 1995), pp. 19–25.

3. Deepak Chopra, *Boundless Energy: The Complete Mind/Body Program for Overcoming Chronic Fatigue* (New York: Harmony Books, 1995), p. 19; see also Lad, pp. 31–35.

4. William Collinge, *The American Holistic Health Association Complete Guide to Alternative Medicine* (New York: Warner Books, 1996), p. 62; Lad, pp. 37–42.

5. Lad, pp. 52–68.

6. Scott Gerson, *Ayurveda: The Ancient Indian Healing Art* (Rockport, Mass.: Element Books, 1993), pp. 56–59; Lad, pp. 88–99B; Collinge, pp. 64–65; Chopra, pp. 53–54.

7. Lad, pp. 129–141; see also Gerson, pp. 89–97.

8. Gerson, p. 101; Lad, pp. 69–70, 75–78; Nancy Lonsdorf et al., *A Woman's Best Medicine: Health, Happiness, and Long Life Through Ayur-Veda* (New York: G. P. Putnam's Sons, 1993), pp. 307–310.

9. Lad, pp. 70–71; Gerson, pp. 101–102.

10. Chopra, pp. 40–41.

11. Lonsdorf et al., p. 241.

12. Lad, pp. 73–75; Gerson, pp. 102–103.

13. Lad, pp. 78–79; Gerson, pp. 103–104.

14. Chopra, pp. 94–95.

15. Lad, pp. 113–122; Collinge, p. 74.

16. Louise Taylor, *A Woman's Book of Yoga: A Journal for Health and Self-Discovery* (Rutland, Vt.: Charles E. Tuttle Company, 1993), pp. 2–3, 38–43, 104, 149, 192.

17. Hari Sharma, *Freedom from Disease* (Toronto, Ont.: Veda, 1993), pp. 279–282; Collinge, pp. 74–75; Taylor, p. 122.

18. Meditation Information Network, at <http://www.minet.org>; Jack Raso, *Mystical Diets: Paranormal, Spiritual, and Occult Nutrition Practices* (Buffalo: Prometheus Books, 1993), p. 94.

19. Kurt Butler, *A Consumer's Guide to Alternative Medicine* (Buffalo: Prometheus Books, 1992), pp. 110–119.

20. Jack Raso, "Alternative Healthcare, Ayurveda, and Neo-Hinduism," Nutrition *Forum*, vol. 11, July–August 1994, p. 31; Raso, *Mystical Diets*, pp. 79–96; Stephen Barrett and William T. Jarvis, eds., *The Health Robbers* (Buffalo: Prometheus Books, 1993), pp. 240–245.

21. Collinge, p. 78.

22. "Acupuncture," *Consumer Reports*, vol. 59, January 1994, p. 54.

23. Luc De Schepper, *Acupuncture in Practice* (Sante Fe: Full of Life Publishing, 1995), pp. 7–10.

24. Ibid., p. 9.

25. Ibid., pp. 11–18.

26. Collinge, pp. 14–22.

27. Leon Chaitow, *The Acupuncture Treatment of Pain* (Rochester, Vt.: Healing Arts Press, 1990), pp. 24–25; Marie Cargill, *Acupuncture: A Viable Medical Alternative* (Westport, Conn.: Praeger, 1994), p. 28.

28. Chaitow, pp. 24–25; Cargill, p. 29.

29. Chaitow, p. 24.

30. De Schepper, pp. 43–58.

31. Carole Rogers, associate professor, University of Technology Sydney College of Acupuncture, E–mail communication, August 20, 1996.

32. Cargill, pp. 28–29.

33. Ibid., p. 21; "Acupuncture FAQ," at <http://www.acupuncture.com>.

34. See, for example, Cargill, pp. 17, 21–23; De Schepper, pp. 109–116.

35. Collinge, pp. 24–26.

36. Ibid., p. 31–32; Cargill, pp. 33–34.

37. Ibid., pp. 29–30.

38. Rogers, E–mail communication.

39. Ibid.

40. Barrett and Jarvis, pp. 259–268.

41. Ibid., pp. 262–264.

42. Ibid., pp. 266–268.

43. Butler, pp. 100–101.

44. Cargill, pp. 37–44.

45. "Acupuncture" (Consumer Reports), p. 54.

46. Collinge, p. 33.

47. Steve Sternberg, "Mainstream U.S. Science Endorses Acupuncture," *USA Today*, November 6, 1997, p. 2D.

48. Rogers, E–mail communication.

Chapter 5. Herbal and Nutritional Therapies

1. In this chapter the word *herbal* refers generally to remedies derived from plants, including those botanically classified as herbs as well as others.

2. Douglas Schar, *The Backyard Medicine Chest: An Herbal Primer* (Washington, D.C.: Elliott & Clark Publishing, 1995), pp. 20–24; see also David Hoffmann, *The Complete Illustrated Holistic Herbal* (Rockport, Mass.: Element Books, 1996), p. 75; "Herbal Roulette," *Consumer Reports*, vol. 60, November 1995, pp. 698, 700–701.

3. Schar, pp. 35–41; see also Lalitha Thomas, *10 Essential Herbs*, 2d ed. (Prescott, Ariz.: Hohm Books, 1996), pp. 245–267.

4. Schar, pp. 41–47; see also "Herbal Roulette" (*Consumer Reports*), pp. 700–701.

5. Hoffman, pp. 136, 207–209; (Hoffman has served as president of the American Herbalist Guild); Richard Mabey et al., *The New Age Herbalist* (New York: Collier Books, Macmillan Publishing Company, 1988), p. 72.

6. Hoffman, pp. 113, 208–209; Mabey et al., p. 68.

7. Hoffman, p. 153, Mabey et al., pp. 72–76.

8. Personal interview, November 2, 1997.

9. Ibid.

10. P. L. LeBars et al., "A Placebo-Controlled, Double-blind, Randomized Trial of an Extract of Ginkgo Biloba for Dementia," *Journal of the American Medical Association*, vol. 278, October 22/29, 1997, p. 1327.

11. Compare Adam Adler and Bruce Holub, "Effect of Garlic and Fish-Oil Supplement on Serum Lipid and Lipoprotein Concentrations in Hypercholesterolemic Men," *American Journal of Clinical Nutrition*, vol. 65, February 1997, p. 445, and Joel Gore and James Dalen, "Cardiovascular Disease," *Journal of the American Medical Association*, vol. 271, June 1, 1994, p. 1660, with "Garlic: Great for Cooking, But Not Much Else," *University of California, Berkeley Wellness Letter*, vol. 12, June 1996, p. 1. See generally, Jean Seligman, "Sex, Lies & Garlic," *Newsweek*, vol. 126, November 6, 1995, p. 65.

12. Cynthia Hochswender, "The Big Nine: An Expert's Guide to Growing and Using the Most Healthful Herbs," *American Health for Women*, vol. 16, June 1997, p. 74; Sharon Doyle Driedger, "Cold Comfort: A Mineral and a Herb Win Supporters in the Battle against the Sniffles," *Maclean's*, vol. 110, February 24, 1997, p. 54; Thomas, pp. 342–353.

13. "How Potent Is Echinacea?" *University of California, Berkeley Wellness Letter*, vol. 10, November 1993, p. 2; Seligman, pp. 65–66; Mabey, p. 45; Jack Wolfe, "Natural-born Healers," *Men's Health*, vol. 11, April 1996, p. 68.

14. Dafna W. Gordon et al., "Chaparral Ingestion: The Broadening Spectrum of Liver Injury Caused by Herbal Medications," *Journal of the American Medical Association*, vol. 273, February 8, 1995, p. 489.

15. Gordon et al.; see also "Are Herbal Remedies

Safe?" *McCall's*, vol. 122, July 1995, p. 40; and "Chaparral Dangerous," *FDA Consumer*, vol. 27, March 1993, p. 4.

16. "Herbal Roulette," pp. 700–701; Mark Teich and Pamela Weintraub, "Are Natural Cures a Prescription for Danger?" *Redbook*, vol. 185, June 1995, pp. 88, 89; Wolfe, pp. 68.

17. See, for example, Mabey et al., pp. 64, 76, 97.

18. Jack Raso, *Mystical Diets: Paranormal, Spiritual, and Occult Nutrition Practices* (Buffalo: Prometheus Books, 1993), p. 228.

19. "Herbal Roulette," (*Consumer Reports*), p. 698; Kurt Butler, *A Consumer's Guide to "Alternative Medicine"* (Buffalo: Prometheus Books, 1993), pp. 192–193.

20. Teich and Weintraub, p. 111, quoting Victor Herbert.

21. Karyn Snyder, "Ecstatic Exit: Sale of Herbal Stimulant Now Banned in Florida," *Drug Topics*, vol. 140, May 20, 1996, p. 40.

22. Doug Levy, "FDA Targets 'Herbal High,'" *USA Today*, August 28, 1996, p. 1A; FDA, *Morbidity and Mortality Weekly Report, On–line Summaries*, August 6, 1996.

23. Ibid.; Mariette DiChristina, "The New Weed," *Popular Science*, vol. 249, August 1996, p. 32; Snyder, p. 40.

24. Carol Schiller and David Schiller, *Aromatherapy Oils: A Complete Guide* (New York: Sterling Publishing Company, 1996), p. 7; Mabey et al., p. 150.

25. Schiller and Schiller, pp. 75–76; Valerie Ann Worwood, *The Complete Book of Essential Oils and Aromatherapy* (San Rafael, Calif.: New World Library,

1991), pp. 19–20; Charla Devereux, *The Aromatherapy Kit: Essential Oils and How to Use Them* (Boston: Charles E. Tuttle Company, 1993), pp. 98–99.

26. Worwood, p. 21; Devereux, p. 98.

27. Worwood, p. 21; Devereux, pp. 99–100; Schiller and Schiller, pp. 96–97.

28. See, for example, Mabey et al., p. 151, Devereux, pp. 35, 38–40, 44.

29. Devereux, pp. 21–22, 65–66; Mabey et al., p. 150.

30. "Aromatherapy: The Nose Knows?" University of California Berkeley Wellness Letter, vol. 11, May 1995, p. 4.

31. Lynn McCutcheon, "What's That I Smell? The Claims of Aromatherapy," *Skeptical Inquirer*, vol. 20, May/June 1996, p. 35. See also Gustav Carsch, "Aromatherapy Revisited," *Soap-Cosmetics-Chemical Specialties*, vol. 70, August 1994, p. 24.

32. Personal interview, November 3, 1997.

33. Jane Heimlich, *What Your Doctor Won't Tell You* (New York: HarperPerennial, 1990), pp. 195–196.

34. These concepts also figure prominently in acupuncture, although in some instances classifications are reversed. See Raso, p. 33.

35. Michio Kushi and Edward Esko, *Holistic Health through Macrobiotics* (New York: Japan Publications, 1993), pp. 17–26, 41–42, 136–140, 249–281.

36. Heimlich, p. 196.

37. See, for example, Kushi and Esko, pp. 149–151; Heimlich, pp. 199–203.

38. Edward Esko, Notes from the *Boundless Frontier: Reflections on the Macrobiotic Diet, Philosophy, and Way of Life* (Becket, Mass.: One Peaceful World Press, 1992), p. 54. See also Anthony J. Satillaro and Tom Monte, *Living Well Naturally* (Boston: Houghton Mifflin Company, 1984), p. 8 (Macrobiotics "doesn't mean we should stop seeing our doctors and begin treating ourselves").

39. Heimlich, p. 205.

40. Albert Marchetti, *Beating the Odds: Alternative Treatments That Have Worked Miracles against Cancer* (Chicago: Contemporary Books, 1988), pp. 96–97.

41. Stephen Barrett and William T. Jarvis, eds., *The Health Robbers* (Buffalo: Prometheus Books, 1993), p. 88.

42. Kushi and Esko, pp. 200–234.

43. Jack Raso, "Virtualistic Gurus and Their Legacies," in *Barrett and Jarvis*, eds., pp. 231–232; Jack Raso, *"Alternative" Healthcare: A Comprehensive Guide* (Buffalo: Prometheus Books, 1994), pp. 83–85.

44. Raso, *Mystical Diets*, p. 42; Raso, "Vitalistic Gurus," p. 233.

45. Jennifer Jacobs, ed., *The Encyclopedia of Alternative Medicine* (Boston: Journey Editions, 1996), p. 89.

46. Kristine Napier, "Too Many Vitamins?" *Harvard Health Letter*, vol. 21, January 1996, p. 1.

47. Heimlich, pp. 106–107, 223–226.

48. Marchetti, pp. 115–117.

49. Ibid., pp. 117–24; Napier, pp. 1–3.

50. Heiner Bucher et al., "Effect of Calcium Supplement on Pregnancy-Induced Hypertension and Preeclampsia," *Journal of the American Medical Association*, vol. 275, April 10, 1996, p. 1113.

51. Conventional and alternative medicine practitioners differ on whether the diet or supplements should be used to provide adequate calcium. See Michele Lesie, "Beating Osteoporosis: Calcium Plays Major Role in Reducing Risk," *Cleveland Plain Dealer*, November 4, 1997, p. 1E.

52. Kristine Napier, "Facts and Fiction about Vitamin E," *Harvard Health Letter*, vol. 22, November 1996, p. 1; Nigel Stevens et al., "Randomised Controlled Trial of Vitamin E in Patients with Coronary Disease: Cambridge Heart Antioxidant Study," *Lancet*, vol. 347, p. 781.

53. Napier, pp. 1–3; Marchetti, pp. 117–122.

54. Larry Clark et al., "Effects of Selenium Supplement for Cancer Prevention in Patients with Carcinoma of the Skin: A Randomized Controlled Trial," *Journal of the American Medical Association*, vol. 276, December 25, 1996, p. 1957; Graham Colditz, "Selenium and Cancer Prevention: Promising Results Indicate Further Trials Required," *Journal of the American Medical Association*, vol. 276, December 25, 1996, p. 1984.

55. Richard Clark et al., "Selenium Poisoning from a Nutritional Supplement," *Journal of the American Medical Association*, vol. 275, April 10, 1996, p. 1087; "Wonder Drug or Poison Pill?" *Insight on the News*, vol. 13, February 17, 1997, p. 44.

56. Napier, pp. 1–3.

57. Raso, *Mystical Diets*, pp. 193–201.

Chapter 6. Healing Hands

1. Janet Macrae, *Therapeutic Touch: A Practical Guide* (New York: Knopf, 1988), pp. 4–6, 22–63.

2. Ibid., pp. 47, 79–80.

3. Ibid., pp. 58–63.

4. William Collinge, *The American Holistic Health Association Complete Guide to Alternative Medicine* (New York: Warner Books, 1996), pp. 232–283, 288–290; Jane Heimlich, *What Your Doctor Won't Tell You* (New York: HarperPerennial, 1990), pp. 251–252.

5. Bela Scheiber and Carla Selby, "UAB Final Report of Therapeutic Touch—An Appraisal," *Skeptical Inquirer*, vol. 21, May/June 1997, p. 53.

6. Stephen Barrett and William T. Jarvis, eds., *The Health Robbers* (Buffalo: Prometheus Books, 1993), p. 364.

7. David Sneed and Sharon Sneed, *The Hidden Agenda: A Critical View of Alternative Medical Therapies* (Nashville: Thomas Nelson, 1991), pp. 170–174. The Sneeds also criticize other alternative therapies that advocate meditation.

8. Robert Glickman and Janet Burns, "If Therapeutic Touch Works, Prove It!" *RN*, vol. 59, December 1996, p. 76.

9. Leon Jaroff, "A No–Touch Therapy," *Time*, vol. 144, November 21, 1994, p. 88.

10. Collinge, pp. 276–277; Jack Raso, *"Alternative" Healthcare A Comprehensive Guide* (Buffalo: Prometheus Books, 1994), p. 118; Jennifer Jacobs, ed., *The Encyclopedia of Alternative Medicine* (Boston: Journey Editions, 1996), pp. 132–135.

11. Raso, *"Alternative" Healthcare*, pp. 220–221, quoting Ida Rolf.

12. Ida P. Rolf, *Rolfing: Reestablishing the Natural Alignment and Structural Integration of the Human Body for Vitality and Well-Being* (Rochester, Vt.: Healing Arts Press, 1989), pp. 25–26.

13. "Rolfing & Rolfing Movement Integration: The Whole Body Approach to Well–Being," (pamphlet, Rolf Institute, Boulder, Colorado, 1991).

14. See generally, Rolf; Jason Mixter, "Rolfing" (pamphlet, Rolf Institute, Boulder, Colorado).

15. Rolf, pp. 275–283; Mixter, pp. 4–6.

16. Raso, "Alternative" *Healthcare*, pp. 118–119.

17. Michael Castleman, *Nature's Cures* (Emmaus, Pa.: Rodale Books, 1996), pp. 24–25.

18. See generally articles and links at <http://www.reflexology.org>.

19. Robert Buckman and Karl Sabbagh, *Magic or Medicine? An Investigation of Healing and Healers* (Amherst, N.Y.: Prometheus Books, 1995), pp. 189–190; John Renner, *HealthSmarts* (Kansas City, Mo.: HealthFacts Publishing), pp. 106–108.

20. Robert Carroll, *The Skeptic's Dictionary*, at <http://dcn.davis.ca.us/~btcarrol/skeptic/dictcont.html>.

Chapter 7. Mind over Matter

1. Bill Moyers, *Healing and the Mind* (New York: Doubleday, 1993), pp. 71–75.

2. Beth Higbee et al., "Healing Currents," *Prevention*, vol. 46, December 1994, pp. 66, 69–70; Jane Heimlich, *What Your Doctor Won't Tell You* (New York: HarperPerennial, 1990), pp. 70–72.

3. Stephen Barrett and William T. Jarvis, eds., *The Health Robbers* (Buffalo: Prometheus Books, 1993), pp. 424–425.

4. Moyers, p. 115.

5. Ibid., p. 119.

6. Ibid., pp. 123–130.

7. Bill Gottlieb, ed., *New Choices in Natural Healing* (Emmaus, Pa.: Rodale Books, 1995), pp. 163–164, describing an exercise recommended by psychiatrist Gerald Epstein.

8. Albert Marchetti, *Beating the Odds: Alternative Treatments That Have Worked Miracles against Cancer* (Chicago: Contemporary Books, 1988), pp. 174–179.

9. See generally, Bernie Siegel, Love, *Medicine and Miracles* (New York: Harper & Row, 1986); Bernie Siegel, *How to Live Between Office Visits* (New York: HarperCollins, 1993). See also Michael Castleman, *Nature's Cures* (Emmaus, Pa.: Rodale Books, 1996), pp. 393–406.

10. Personal interviews, 1988–1989.

11. Robert Buckman and Karl Sabbagh, *Magic or Medicine? An Investigation of Healing and Healers* (Amherst, N.Y.: Prometheus Books, 1995), pp. 98–99, 236–227.

12. David Sneed and Sharon Sneed, *The Hidden Agenda: A Critical View of Alternative Medical Therapies* (Nashville: Thomas Nelson, 1991), pp. 26–28, 74.

13. Belleruth Naparstek, *Staying Well with Guided Imagery* (New York: Warner Books, 1994), pp. 6–15.

14. Ibid., pp. 93–99.

15. "Parents Are Tried in Death," *Cleveland Plain Dealer*, January 22, 1987, p. 2B. The judge later dismissed the charges because he struck down part

of the law, and another bill was swiftly introduced in the Ohio legislature to require parents to obtain medical attention for children, regardless of their religious beliefs. See "Faith Healers Cleared; But Judge Strikes Down Law," *Cleveland Plain Dealer*, April 28, 1987, p. 1B.

16. For Christian Scientist case histories, see Fred Frohock, *Healing Powers: Alternative Medicine, Spiritual Communities, and the State* (Chicago: University of Chicago Press, 1992), pp. 251–266.

17. See generally, Barrett and Jarvis, pp. 340–343. See also Sneed and Sneed, pp. 36–37, 119–124, arguing that it is arrogant to "demand healing from God on your own arbitrary terms."

18. Barrett and Jarvis, pp. 344–345.

19. Ibid., pp. 337–340; 343–345.

20. David M. Eisenberg et al., "Unconventional Medicine in the United States—Prevalence, Costs, and Patterns of Use," *New England Journal of Medicine*, vol. 328, January 28, 1993, pp. 246–249.

21. Castleman, *Nature's Cures*, pp. 400–401.

22. Personal interviews, June–July 1996.

Chapter 8. Making Decisions

1. William Collinge, *The American Holistic Health Association Complete Guide to Alternative Medicine* (New York: Warner Books, 1996), pp. 100–103; Jack Raso, *"Alternative" Healthcare: A Comprehensive Guide* (Buffalo: Prometheus Books, 1994), pp. 101–104.

2. Workshop on Alternative Medicine, *Alternative Medicine: Expanding Medical Horizons*. Report to the National Institutes of Health (Washington, D.C.: Government Printing Office, 1994), pp. xxvii–xxxi.

3. Collinge, p. 33.

4. Marilyn Elias, "A Mind for Health: Clearer Link Between the Head and Healing," *USA Today*, March 31, 1997, p. 1D, quoting Rep. DeFazio at p. 2D.

5. Michael Castleman, "Medical Breakthroughs: New Ways Doctors Heal," *Family Circle*, vol. 109, November 1, 1996, p. 44, quoting Dr. Jonas at p. 46.

6. Elias, p. 2D.

7. Stephen Barrett and William T. Jarvis, eds., *The Health Robbers* (Buffalo: Prometheus Books, 1993), pp. 94–99.

8. Ibid., pp. 94–99, 409–415.

9. Pete Williams, "Comeback against Cancer," *USA Today Baseball Weekly*, August 28–September 3, 1996, p. 16, quoting a Los Angeles Dodgers outfielder at p. 18.

10. Paula Kurtzweil, "A 'Washed-Up' Snake-Oil Scheme," *FDA Consumer*, vol. 30, September 1996, p. 30.

11. Quackery Immunization Kids," *FDA Press Release P89–48*, November 15, 1989.

12. Isadora Stehlin, "An FDA Guide to Choosing Medical Treatments," *FDA Consumer*, vol. 29, June 1995, p. 10.

13. E-mail correspondence from Robert Carroll, September 14, 1996.

14. Ibid.

15. Carolyn Gard, "Beware of Health Frauds Aimed at Teens," *Current Health 2*, vol. 22, April, 1996, p. 30; see also Stehlin, p. 13.

16. Gard, p. 31.

17. "FDA and Top Health Frauds," *FDA Backgrounder*, March 1990.

18. David M. Eisenberg et al., "Unconventional Medicine in the United States—Prevalence, Costs, and Patterns of Use," *New England Journal of Medicine*, vol. 328, January 28, 1993, pp. 251–252.

Index